earthworks

3

John Widdowson

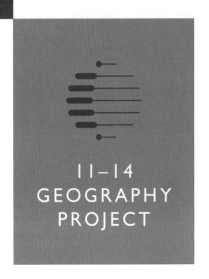

11–14
GEOGRAPHY
PROJECT

HODDER
EDUCATION
AN HACHETTE UK COMPANY

Contents

UNIT 1

EARTHQUAKES AND VOLCANOES – CAN PEOPLE PREPARE FOR DISASTERS?   1

UNIT 2

DEVELOPMENT – IS THERE MORE TO IT THAN MONEY?   23

UNIT 3

CITIES – CAN YOU SEE THE PATTERNS?   45

earthworks
3

Author's acknowledgements

The author would like to thank the following people who have all contributed to *Earthworks 3*: Catherine Hurst, Keith Mears, Andy Schofield, Jeff Stanfield, Andrew Stacey and Steve Thomas for all their helpful ideas and criticism; Samantha Chuula and Alan Widdowson, who carried out research in Zambia and the USA; Mark and Joanne Potterton, Mary van der Reit and Sbongile Madolo, who made me welcome in South Africa and made my trip such a success; and finally the many people around the world who agreed to be photographed and interviewed and who appear in this book.

First published 2000
by Hodder an Hachette UK Company,
338 Euston Road,
London NW1 3BH

Reprinted 2000, 2002, 2003, 2004, 2005, 2007, 2008, 2009, 2011

Artwork by Oxford Illustrators Ltd
Layouts by Amanda Easter
Cover design by John Townson, Creation
Typeset in Sabon 11½/13pt by Wearset, Boldon, Tyne & Wear
Printed and bound by Oriental Press, Dubai

A CIP catalogue record for this book is available from the British Library.

ISBN-13: 978 0 719 57074 2
Teacher's Resource Book ISBN 978 0 7195 7075 9

UNIT 4
UNIT 5
UNIT 6

About Earthworks

In *Earthworks 3* there are six units and a section focusing on the USA. Each unit covers a different geographical theme or country. You will notice that the units follow a similar pattern, and have the same features.

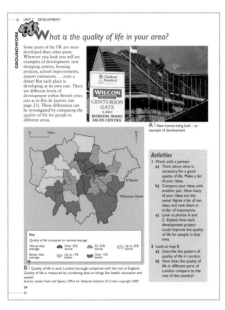

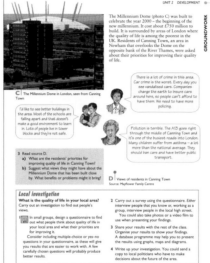

GROUNDWORK – an introduction to the unit, based on your everyday experience of geography.

Local investigation
These are investigations that you can do with the rest of your class in your own local area, or as part of a geography field trip.

FRAMEWORK – covers all the key geographical ideas that you need to understand in the unit.

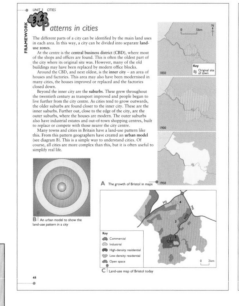

Key words
New geographical words are printed in **bold** letters. These are words that you really need to know. The glossary at the back of the book includes these words, and tells you their meanings. You will probably find it helpful to keep your own dictionary of these words as you go through the book.

Homework
This is an activity that you could do at home. It often involves doing some extra research on your own.

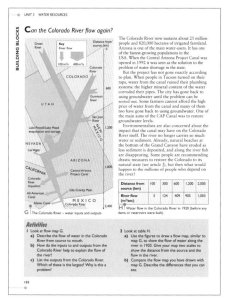

BUILDING BLOCKS – two or three geographical investigations, based on the *Framework* ideas, using real places.

Assignment
This is an extended activity where you are expected to use many of the geographical skills and ideas from the unit.

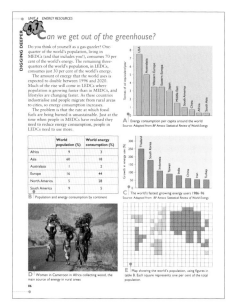

This symbol shows the best opportunities to use a computer to help you with the activities you do. But they are not the only opportunities. There are many ways that computers can help you learn about geography.

DIGGING DEEPER – an in-depth look at a topical issue, to take your geography that little bit further.

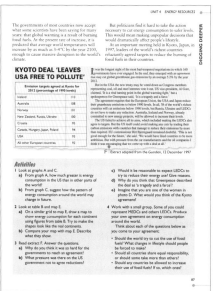

Activities
You can do most of these in your class, either on your own, or in a group. They often involve writing or drawing, but looking and thinking are important activities too.

Acknowledgements

The Publishers would like to thank the following for permission to reproduce copyright material:
p.3 the *Guardian*, 4 June 1998 and 20 July 1998; **p.24** *London Facts and Figures*, Office for National Statistics © Crown copyright 2000; **p.25** Mayflower Family Centre; **p.26** World Bank, 1998; **p.34** World Bank 1998; UNDP 1996; **p.40** Oxfam; International Coffee Organisation; The Fairtrade Foundation; **p.46** John Moores University, Liverpool; **p.53** Reproduced from the Ordnance Survey 1:50,000 Landranger mapping with the permission of the Controller of Her Majesty's Stationery Office © Crown copyright (399604); **p.55** Bristol City Council, *Ward Report*, 1991; **p.66** adapted from the *Guardian*, 17 October 1998; **p.78** Reproduced from the Ordnance Survey 1:50,000 Landranger mapping with the permission of the Controller of Her Majesty's Stationery Office © Crown copyright (399604); **p.86** *BP Amoco Statistical Review of World Energy*; **p.87** adapted from the *Guardian*, 12 December 1997; **p.98** Reproduced from the Ordnance Survey 1:50,000 Landranger mapping with the permission of the Controller of Her Majesty's Stationery Office © Crown copyright (399604); **p.103** *World Rivers Review*; **pp.116–7, 120, 124, 130** Statistics South Africa.

Every effort has been made to trace all copyright holders, but if any have been inadvertently overlooked the publishers will be pleased to make the necessary arrangement at the first opportunity.

Photo credits

Cover *t* © Tony Stone Images/David Schultz, *cl* The Stock Market, *c* John Widdowson, *bl* © Tony Stone Images/G. Brad Lewis, *bc* © Tony Stone Images/David Woodfall, *br* Mark Edwards/Still Pictures; **p.iv** *t* © J.L. Atlan/Corbis Sygma, *c* John Maier/Still Pictures, *b* Aerofilms; **p.v** *t* Copyright W.T. Sullivan III/Science Photo Library, *c* Shehzad Noorani/Still Pictures, *b* John Widdowson; **p.1** © J.L. Atlan/Corbis Sygma; **p.2** Marc Deville/Gamma/Frank Spooner Pictures; **p.4** Iwase/Sipa Press/Rex Features; **p.5** © Patrick Robert/Corbis Sygma; **p.6** Geospace/Science Photo Library; **p.7** *l* © Douglas Peebles/Robert Harding Picture Library, *r* Rex Features; **p.8** Andrew Lambert; **p.9** *t* Photri/Robert Harding Picture Library, *b* Gerard & Margi Moss/Still Pictures; **p.12** *t* John Widdowson, *b* Robert Harding Picture Library; **p.14** John Widdowson; **p.15** *l* Sipa Press/Rex Features, *r* © Chloe Harford/Corbis Sygma; **p.16** McDermott/Sipa Press/Rex Features; **p.17** *t* Kevin Schafer/Still Pictures, *b* Butler/Bauer/Rex Features; **p.19** © G. Hellier/Robert Harding Picture Library; **p.20** *t* Science Photo Library, *b* Dr Ken MacDonald/Science Photo Library; **p.22** *t* Chris James/Still Pictures, *cl* © Travel Ink/Chris North, *cr* The Natural History Museum, London, *b* Geoscience Features Picture Library; **p.23** John Maier/Still Pictures; **p.24** Dylan Garcia/Still Pictures; **p.25** John Widdowson; **p.26** *l* Polak/Corbis Sygma, *r* Jorgen Schytte/Still Pictures; **p.28** Mary Evans Picture Library; **p.29** © Richard Greenhill/Sally & Richard Greenhill Photo Library; **p.30** Patrick Lucero/Rex Features; **p.31** Shehzad Noorani/Still Pictures; **p.32** *both* Samantha Chuula; **p. 33** *t* Samantha Chuula, *b* © David Keith Jones/Images of Africa Photobank; **p.34** Mark Edwards/Still Pictures; **p.35** © Richard Greenhill/Sally & Richard Greenhill Photo Library; **p.39** Simon Fraser/Rex Features; **p.40** *t* John Widdowson, *b* John Townson/Creation; **p.41** Nigel Dickinson/Still Pictures; **p.42** © Sally & Richard Greenhill/Sally & Richard Greenhill Photo Library; **p.44** *l* © Trygve Bølstad/Panos Pictures, *r* Ron Giling/Still Pictures; **p.45** Aerofilms; **p.46** *t* David Hartley/Rex Features; **p.47** © John Walmsley; **p.49** *t, ct & b* John Widdowson, *cb* Rex Features; **p.50** Popperfoto; **p.51** © Richard Greenhill/Sally & Richard Greenhill Photo Library; **p.52** *all* John Widdowson; **p.54** *t* © Rob Cousins/Robert Harding Picture Library, *c* John Widdowson, *b* © Sealand Aerial Photography; **p.56** © Sealand Aerial Photography; **p.57** © Sealand Aerial Photography; **p.58** *both* John Widdowson; **p.59** *t* Clive Dixon/Rex Features, *b* John Widdowson; **p.60** Popperfoto; **p.61** © Travel Ink/Abbie Enock; **p.62** © Michael J. Howell/Robert Harding Picture Library; **p.63** *t* © John van Hasselt/Corbis Sygma, *b* © Ecoscene; **p.64** © Sally Greenhill/Sally & Richard Greenhill Photo Library; **p.65** *t* © Skyscan Photolibrary, *b* John Townson/Creation; **p.66** Manni Mason's Pictures; **p.67** Copyright W.T. Sullivan III/Science Photo Library; **p.68** John Townson/Creation; **p.69** Robert Henno/Still Pictures; **p.70** John Townson/Creation; **p.71** Fred Dott/Still Pictures; **p.72** *t* Mark Edwards/Still Pictures, *b* Jim Wark/Still Pictures; **p.73** *t* Klaus Andrews/Still Pictures, *b* Mark Edwards/Still Pictures; **p.74** © Ecoscene/Angela Hampton; **p.75** *t* © Tom Van Sant/Geosphere Project, Santa Monica/Science Photo Library, *b* Nigel Dickinson/Still Pictures; **p.76** Mark Edwards/Still Pictures; **p.77** *l* © Richard Greenhill/Sally & Richard Greenhill Photo Library, *r* Chris James/Still Pictures; **p.78** © Travel Ink/Andrew Watson; **p.79** *t* David Drain/Still Pictures, *b* Peter Brooker/Rex Features; **p.80** *l* Mark Edwards/Still Pictures, *r* David Drain/Still Pictures; **p.81** *t* © H. David Seawell/Corbis, *b* US Geological Survey/Science Photo Library; **p.82** Robert Harding Picture Library; **p.83** Alan Widdowson; **p.84** *t* Al Grillo/Still Pictures, *b* Mark Edwards/Still Pictures; **p.86** Mark Edwards/Still Pictures; **p.88** *t* Hartmut Schwarzbach/Still Pictures, *b* Joerg Boethling/Still Pictures; **p.89** *t* © Ecoscene/Andrew Brown, *b* Shehzad Noorani/Still Pictures; **p.90** © Ecoscene/Anthony Cooper; **p.91** Mark Edwards/Still Pictures; **p.93** © Skyscan Photolibrary; **p.94** Jorgen Schytte/Still Pictures; **p.97** *both* © Thames Water; **p.100** *both* © Ecoscene/Sally Morgan; **p.101** *both* Alan Widdowson; **p.103** J.P. Delobelle/Still Pictures; **p.105** *both* © Sarah Errington/Hutchison Library; **p.107** *l* © G. Hellier/Robert Harding Picture Library, *cl* © Travel Ink/Abbie Enock, *cr* Alan Widdowson, *r* © Ecoscene/Andrew Brown; **p.111** John Widdowson; **p.112** *l* Camera Press, *r* John Widdowson; **p.114** *t* © David C. Williams/Images of Africa Photobank, *b* © Friedrich von Hörsten/Images of Africa Photobank; **p.116** *tl, bl & br* John Widdowson, *tr* Mykel Nicolaou/Link ©; **p.117** Paddy Donnelly/Panos Pictures; **p.118** *l* Popperfoto, *r* © Ingrid Hudson/Hutchison Library; **p.119** Patrick Drand/Corbis Sygma; **p.121** *both* John Widdowson; **p.122** John Widdowson; **p.123** *all* John Widdowson; **p.124** *both* John Widdowson; **p.125** John Widdowson; **p.126** *both* John Widdowson; **p.127** John Widdowson; **p.128** John Widdowson; **p.129** Umthathi Training Project; **p.132** *all* John Widdowson.

t = top, *c* = centre, *l* = left, *b* = bottom, *r* = right.

EARTHQUAKES AND VOLCANOES –
Can people prepare for disasters?

Earthquake damage in California

California, on the west coast of the USA, frequently suffers from **earthquakes**. In 1989 there was a major earthquake in San Francisco, the biggest since 1906. It caused this elevated highway to collapse.

- What earthquake damage can you see in the photo?
- Why do you think some roads and buildings were damaged and others were not?
- From the evidence in the photo, would you say that San Francisco was prepared or unprepared for an earthquake?
- How would you feel if you lived in San Francisco?

GROUNDWORK

1.1 Disasters in the news

In Britain we are fortunate that earthquakes are rare and usually very minor. Britain *is* affected by other **natural hazards**, like floods and storms, but they rarely kill many people. In some places, however, natural hazards cause disasters, sometimes killing thousands of people.

Whether a hazard is a disaster depends on where it happens.

The USA is a rich, developed country. Parts of the USA have frequent earthquakes. In 1989 San Francisco experienced a powerful earthquake (see page 1). Sixty-seven people died and over three thousand were injured. Compare that with the effects of the earthquake in India shown in photo A. This was less powerful than the quake which shook San Francisco in 1989. Yet 20,000 people died and hundreds of thousands were injured. Some of the bodies of those that died were never found.

A Devastation caused in Khillari near Mumbai (Bombay) by an earthquake in India in 1993. One-third of the population of this village died.

Activities

I a) Read the list of hazards and disasters in the box below. If there are any words you don't know, look them up in a dictionary.

air crash	avalanche	drought	earthquake
epidemic	explosion	famine	fire flood
forest fire	hurricane	landslide	tidal wave
tornado	volcanic eruption	war	

b) Make two lists:
i) natural hazards
ii) hazards caused by people.
You can include some hazards in both lists.

c) Choose one hazard from each list. Explain why you put each one in that list.

2 Read the text above and look at photo A and the photo on page 1.

a) Compare the impact of the earthquakes in India and the USA.

b) Why might they have had such a different impact? Think about time of day, building design, transport and emergency services.

c) Do you think that earthquakes should be called 'natural disasters'? Explain your answer.

Homework

3 Find out about one disaster that has happened this week. Where did it happen? What happened? Did people die? How many? What other damage was done? How did people cope?

Watching disasters

We get used to seeing disasters on the TV and in our newspapers. In fact, they happen so often that many get only a small amount of attention, and some may never be mentioned. The 1989 earthquake in San Francisco was front page news for several days, but the earthquake near Mumbai in 1993 was not a big news story in British newspapers. Earthquakes are frequent events in California and in India – so why the difference?

Up to 120 dead and hundreds injured as train ploughs into bridge

High-speed carnage

'This shakes me to the core. I had to collect legs and arms from men, women and children. I've never seen anything like this.'
Fireman Walter Streetitmann

'Two minutes before the accident I heard a tremendous rattling and shaking.'
Survivor Wolf-Ruediger Schliebener

B | Front page

The *Guardian*, 20 July 1998

It was 7 p.m. on Friday and dark when a series of harbour waves, or **tsunami**, flattened a tropical paradise ... Seven villages were wiped out and 2,000 died on Papua New Guinea's north coast.

The *Guardian*, 4 June 1998

The German high-speed express was five hours into its journey from Munich to Hamburg when it came off the rails at 125 miles per hour.

First a roar, then the wall of water hit paradise

Christopher Zinn on waves that left 2,000 feared dead in Papua New Guinea

C | Inside page

---

4 Look at newspaper cuttings B and C. They are too small for you to read. They show two disasters treated in different ways by the same newspaper.

a) Read the two paragraphs from the cuttings. Were these natural disasters?

b) Locate the two places on a world map with the help of an atlas.

c) Describe how the newspaper treated each disaster. What similarities and what differences do you notice?

d) Suggest reasons for the different treatment of each disaster. (Papua New Guinea is a long way from Britain, but if a similar disaster happened in Australia how do you think it would be treated?)

5 Collect newspapers in your classroom over a few weeks.

a) In groups, find a range of stories that are about disasters. If you have done homework activity 3 you will have already found some.

Locate each place on a world map with the help of an atlas.

b) Make your own map to show the location of the disasters. How are they distributed around the world?

6 In pairs, analyse some of the newspaper stories to compare the way disasters in rich, more developed countries (mainly in Europe and North America) and disasters in poor, less developed countries (mainly in Asia, Africa and South America) are treated.

a) Consider:

- how much space they take on the page
- where in the newspaper the stories are found
- any differences in the way they are written.

b) Try to explain your observations. Your answers to activity 4d may help you.

1.2 Earthquake!

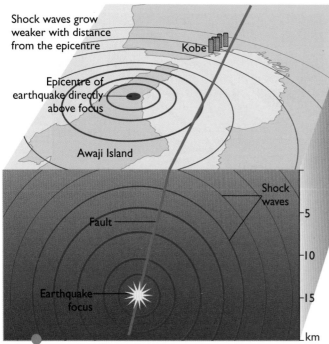

Shock waves grow weaker with distance from the epicentre

Kobe

Epicentre of earthquake directly above focus

Awaji Island

Shock waves

Fault

Earthquake focus

5

10

15

km

A The Kobe earthquake

0	No ground movement
1	
2	
3	
4	
5	
6	
7	
8	
9	
10	No earthquake this strong has ever been recorded

B The Richter scale

At 5.46 a.m. on Tuesday 17 January 1995 an earthquake hit the port city of Kobe in Japan. It measured 7.2 on the **Richter scale** – a scale used to measure the strength of earthquakes (see B below). Japan suffers frequent earthquakes, but this was devastating even by Japan's standards. Over 5,000 people were killed and 100,000 homes were destroyed or badly damaged by the earthquake. Damage costing billions of pounds was done to buildings, roads and railways.

As with most earthquakes, there was no warning. One moment people were asleep in bed, the next they felt as if they were on a roller-coaster, as the floor turned to jelly. Everywhere there was a deafening roar as the ground shook and buildings collapsed.

Kobe was the city closest to the **epicentre** of the earthquake. It was hit by the strongest **shock waves**, but the earthquake was felt less strongly in cities further away. The **focus**, or origin, of the quake was 14 kilometres below the Earth's surface. Here, a sudden movement along a **fault**, or crack in the rock, caused the ground to judder and send out the huge shock waves.

C A double-decker highway in Kobe that collapsed during the earthquake

D   Earthquake damage in Kobe

Activities

I Look at drawing A.
   a) Describe the location of the epicentre of the earthquake.
   b) Explain why Kobe was the Japanese city worst affected by the earthquake.
   c) Use an atlas to name other cities in Japan where the earthquake might have been felt.

2 Look at source B.
   a) Write three sentences describing the effects of earthquakes measuring 3, 5 and 7 on the Richter scale.
   b) What did the Kobe earthquake measure on the Richter scale? How does this account for the amount of damage caused?

3 Look at photos C and D, and the e-mail letters in source E. Describe at least five problems faced by people in Kobe after the earthquake. For each problem state the source of your evidence.

4 Suggest why each of the following happened:
   a) railways closed
   b) there was no water or gas supply
   c) fires started
   d) some houses were destroyed but apartment blocks were not.

Homework

5 Drop a stone into a pond or a bath full of water.
   a) Describe what you see happening on the surface of the water.
   b) What does this tell you about the shock waves from an earthquake?

Thank you for your kindness to send us such messages. This is my first time to experience an earthquake. Though my flat is okay, there are many people who lost their houses, children or parents. Outside I can see a lot of houses broke down and it looks terrible. Now there is no water or gas, also we cannot use any railways.

We are living in the central part of Kobe. It was the most important and busy area, but it isn't now. Many buildings and highways fell down. There were enormous fires in some parts of Kobe. We have food now, sent from many places, but we can't use the toilet or take a bath easily. We are worried that another big earthquake may come again.

We are fine but we don't have water nor gas. I live on the 11th floor of an apartment building. When the earthquake happened, the building was shaken more than a house. I was scared. Many wooden houses were destroyed, so we think in future there will be more apartment buildings.

E   E-mails from school students in Kobe

FRAMEWORK

1.3 Volcanoes

A Mount Etna, a volcano on the Italian island of Sicily, seen from a satellite. The crater of the volcano is near the centre.

ITALY

Sicily ▲ Mt Etna

Volcanoes are formed when **magma**, or molten rock, deep inside the Earth is forced up to the surface through a **vent**, or opening. When the volcano erupts, magma comes to the surface and is then called **lava**. This lava may flow over the surface before it cools and solidifies. **Ash** and **volcanic bombs** may be blown out of the volcano's **crater** into the atmosphere, together with steam and gas.

Over time, layers of lava and ash can build up to form a volcanic **cone**. Smaller vents may branch off from the main vent to form **subsidiary cones**. Mount Etna (photo A) was formed in this way. But volcanoes come in various shapes and sizes. The shape of a volcano and the way that it erupts depend on the type of lava that it produces.

Mount Etna is an **active** volcano which, on average, erupts every few years. After many years lava from the volcano forms fertile soil for farming. Although about a million people live in the area around Mount Etna, few have been killed by the volcano.

Dormant volcanoes can be more dangerous. They may be quiet for hundreds of years, then erupt violently without warning.

Volcanoes that have not erupted for thousands of years and are said to be **extinct**.

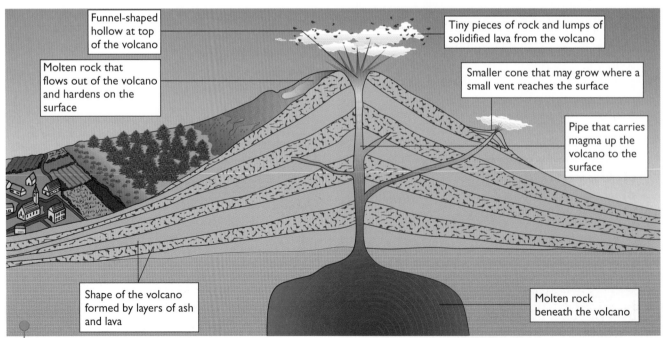

Funnel-shaped hollow at top of the volcano

Molten rock that flows out of the volcano and hardens on the surface

Tiny pieces of rock and lumps of solidified lava from the volcano

Smaller cone that may grow where a small vent reaches the surface

Pipe that carries magma up the volcano to the surface

Shape of the volcano formed by layers of ash and lava

Molten rock beneath the volcano

B Cross-section of a volcano

C A lava flow from Kilauea on Hawaii in the Pacific Ocean, an active volcano that erupts many times each year. The lava is runny and forms a gently sloping mountain, or **shield volcano**.

D An ash cloud from the eruption of Mount St Helens in 1980. The volcano had been dormant for hundreds of years. The lava is very thick, which caused the volcano to explode when it erupted. It forms a steep-sided cone volcano.

Activities

1 Look at drawing B. Read the labels which describe the parts of a volcano.
   a) Match each description on the drawing to a bold word in the first two paragraphs on page 6.
   b) Draw your own cross-section of a volcano and label it using the correct words.

2 Look at satellite photo A.
   a) Use this colour key to work out what you can see in the photo:

   ■ = lava flow/bare rock
   ▨ = natural vegetation
   ⬝ = snow
   ▧ = settlement
   ▦ = farmland.

   b) Draw a sketch map of Mount Etna showing the main areas of each land use.
   c) Describe the pattern shown on your map. How do you explain it?

3 Read the following sentences from a scientist's diary. They describe what happened during an eruption of Mount Etna, but they have been muddled up.

a) Put the sentences in order.

> Red-hot ash was thrown high into the air like a firework display.
> Trees and farmland in the path of the lava were destroyed.
> There was a huge explosion deep inside the volcano.
> The volcano was rumbling and steaming as it does most of the time.
> The lava thickened and slowed down and finally turned to solid rock.
> The whole area was covered in a thin layer of ash as the cloud settled.
> Suddenly the volcano became quiet and stopped steaming.
> Lava poured out of the crater and began to flow down the side of the cone.

b) Compare Mount Etna with the volcanoes in photos C and D. Which volcano do you think is:
i) most dangerous
ii) most predictable?
Give reasons for your answers.

7

In this Building Block you will investigate where around the world earthquakes and volcanoes happen and try to explain the pattern.

1.4 Where do earthquakes and volcanoes happen?

> I think that earthquakes and volcanoes only happen in hot places. The heat cracks the ground.

> I think that they only happen on large continents. Britain is an island, and we don't get earthquakes or volcanoes.

> They only happen in poor countries. People don't have the technology to prevent them.

> I think you can get earthquakes and volcanoes anywhere – it's just a question of luck.

A

Earthquake	Year	Latitude	Longitude
Tangshan (China)	1976	40 °N	118 °E
Mexico City (Mexico)	1985	20 °N	100 °W
Spitak (Armenia)	1988	41 °N	44 °E
San Francisco (USA)	1989	38 °N	122 °W
Northern Iran	1990	39 °N	48 °E
Central India	1993	19 °N	75 °E
Kobe (Japan)	1995	35 °N	135 °E
North-west Turkey	1999	41 °N	30 °E

B Some major earthquakes in recent years

Volcano	Year	Latitude	Longitude
Mount St Helens (USA)	1980	46 °N	122 °W
Nevado del Ruiz (Colombia)	1985	5 °N	76 °W
Soufriere Hills (Montserrat)	1995	16 °N	62 °W
Grimsvötn (Iceland)	1996	65 °N	17 °W
Ruapehu (New Zealand)	1997	39 °S	175 °E
Popocatepetl (Mexico)	1998	19 °N	98 °W
Mount Etna (Italy)	Often	37 °N	15 °E
Kilauea (Hawaii)	Often	20 °N	155 °W

C Volcanic eruptions in recent years

Activities

1 Look at the ideas around photo A.
   a) What do you think about these ideas? Are they right or wrong? Provide evidence to support your opinions.
   b) Write your own hypothesis (or idea) to suggest where earthquakes and volcanoes happen, and why. You will test this hypothesis through the rest of this Building Block to see if it fits the evidence.

2 Look at tables B and C.
   a) Find each of the places in the tables in your atlas. Use the latitude and longitude to find the exact locations.
   b) Locate and mark each one on a blank map of the world.

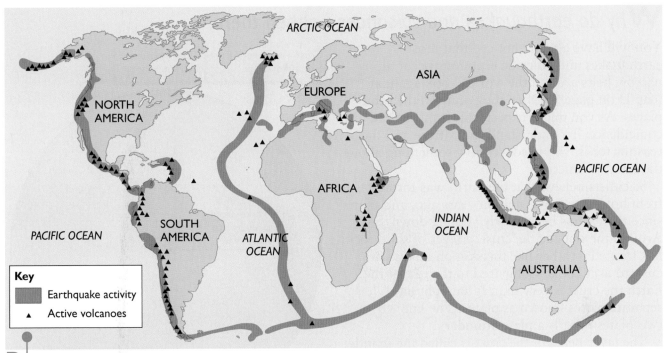

D | Areas of the world where there are earthquakes and volcanic eruptions

E | The aftermath of an earthquake in Alaska

F | A volcanic island in Indonesia

3 a) Find a website on the Internet that has up-to-date information about volcanic eruptions and earthquakes. Try Volcano World: http://volcano.und.nodak.edu/ and National Earthquake Information Center (USA): http://earthquake.usgs.gov/
Have there been any eruptions or earthquakes this week? This month? This year?
Where have they happened?

b) Add any new information you find to your world map.

4 Look at map D.

a) Compare map D to your own map of earthquakes and volcanic eruptions. What do you notice?

b) Describe the pattern on map D. Name the areas where earthquakes and volcanic eruptions happen.

5 a) Look back at the ideas around photo A. Use information on these two pages to disprove each of the ideas.

b) Look again at your own hypothesis about where and why earthquakes and volcanoes happen. Does the information on these pages help to prove or disprove it?

c) Now that you know more, do you need to rewrite your hypothesis? If so, do so now.

BUILDING BLOCKS

Why do earthquakes and volcanoes happen there?

You will have already noticed that most earthquakes and volcanic eruptions occur along narrow belts around the world. Look again at map D on page 9. Often they occur in the same places. As you might expect, this is more than just coincidence. To understand the pattern and the reasons for it, you need to know something about the Earth's structure.

Scientists believe that the Earth was formed from hot gases 4,600 million years ago, and that since then it has been slowly cooling down. Around the outside the **crust**, a layer of solid rock, has formed – rather like the skin on a bowl of custard as it cools. Compared to the rest of the Earth the crust is very thin. It has split into separate pieces known as **plates**. The line where two plates meet is a **plate boundary**.

The layer beneath the crust is called the **mantle**. The plates float like rafts on top of this mantle, where the rock is so hot that it is molten (like treacle). Heat from the solid **core** rises through the mantle creating currents that make the plates above move very slowly – usually no more than a few centimetres each year. Plates can move apart, collide or slide past each other.

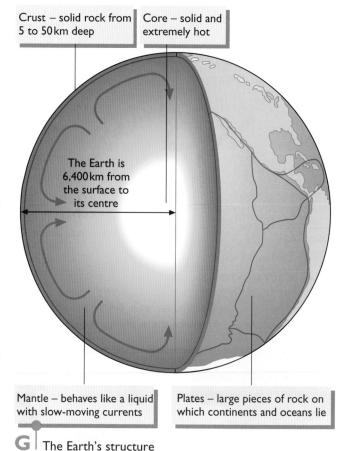

Crust – solid rock from 5 to 50 km deep

Core – solid and extremely hot

The Earth is 6,400 km from the surface to its centre

Mantle – behaves like a liquid with slow-moving currents

Plates – large pieces of rock on which continents and oceans lie

G | The Earth's structure

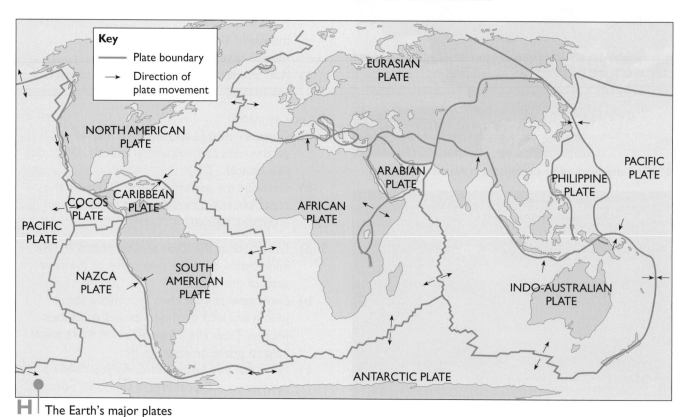

Key

⎯⎯ Plate boundary

⟶ Direction of plate movement

EURASIAN PLATE

NORTH AMERICAN PLATE

PACIFIC PLATE

ARABIAN PLATE

PHILIPPINE PLATE

COCOS PLATE

CARIBBEAN PLATE

AFRICAN PLATE

PACIFIC PLATE

NAZCA PLATE

SOUTH AMERICAN PLATE

INDO-AUSTRALIAN PLATE

ANTARCTIC PLATE

H | The Earth's major plates

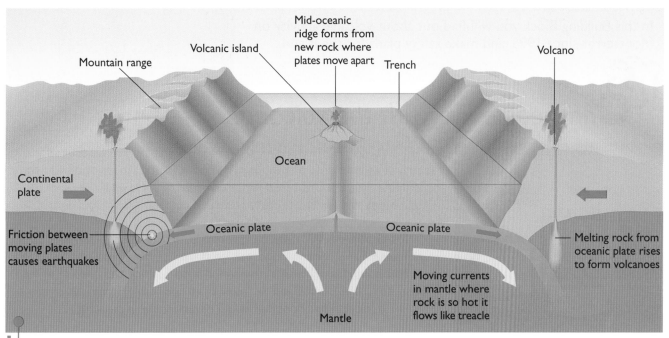

Mountain range

Volcanic island

Mid-oceanic ridge forms from new rock where plates move apart

Trench

Volcano

Continental plate

Ocean

Oceanic plate

Oceanic plate

Friction between moving plates causes earthquakes

Melting rock from oceanic plate rises to form volcanoes

Moving currents in mantle where rock is so hot it flows like treacle

Mantle

I Cross-section of the Earth's crust

Activities

1 Look at drawing G. This shows the Earth's structure in three dimensions. Draw a cross-section of the Earth. Use the information on drawing G to make each layer the correct depth. Give your cross-section a scale.

2 Look at map H. Notice the arrows that show the direction the plates are moving.
   a) Your teacher will give you jigsaw pieces of the Earth's plates. Make up the jigsaw to form a map of the world, and stick the pieces down.
   b) Colour over the plate boundaries. Use three colours to show:

   i) boundaries where plates move apart
   ii) boundaries where plates collide
   iii) boundaries where plates slide past each other.
   c) Compare your map with map D on page 9. Describe what you notice.

3 Look at drawing I.
   a) Explain why:
      i) earthquakes   ii) volcanoes
      are often found near plate boundaries.
   b) How does this help to explain your observations in activity 2c?

Assignment

Where do earthquakes and volcanoes happen?

Look back at your hypothesis. You tried to explain where and why earthquakes and volcanoes happen.

   How close was your hypothesis to the reasons given on these two pages?

   Write one or two paragraphs to evaluate your hypothesis.

• What were you right about?
• What were you wrong about?

Give evidence to show why your ideas were right or wrong.

   Do you need to rewrite your hypothesis now? If so, how would you rewrite it?

Extra

Think about the explanations on these pages of why earthquakes and volcanic eruptions happen in certain places. Can you be sure that they are true? How? What further evidence would you need to prove them?

   (You can find out more in Digging Deeper on pages 20–22.)

In this Building Block you will find out about volcanic activity on Montserrat since 1995, and make safety plans for the island.

1.5 Can people live with the volcano?

Chander Maze

Until 1995 I lived in the town of Plymouth on the Caribbean island of Montserrat. It was one of the prettiest places that you could imagine. Houses clustered around the little port, with the deep blue sea stretching into the distance, and the lush green Soufriere Hills rising beyond.

Not that we didn't have our problems. In 1989 the island was badly damaged by Hurricane Hugo, but that had all been repaired. By 1995 we had a new library and a new hospital to replace the ones that had been destroyed. Little did we know that the library would never see a book and the hospital would never receive a patient . . .

A The Caribbean

Montserrat is one of the Leeward Islands, a chain of islands that have formed where the Atlantic Plate and Caribbean Plate have collided.

B Plymouth, with the Soufriere Hills in the background

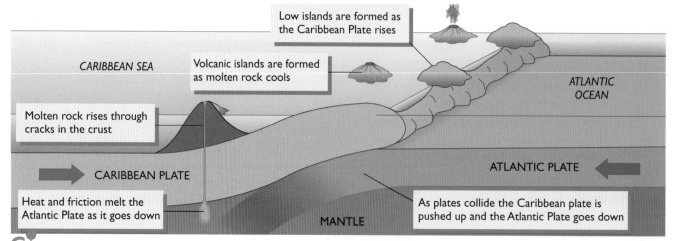

Low islands are formed as the Caribbean Plate rises

CARIBBEAN SEA

Volcanic islands are formed as molten rock cools

ATLANTIC OCEAN

Molten rock rises through cracks in the crust

CARIBBEAN PLATE

ATLANTIC PLATE

Heat and friction melt the Atlantic Plate as it goes down

As plates collide the Caribbean plate is pushed up and the Atlantic Plate goes down

MANTLE

C Island formation in the Caribbean

. . . because on 18 July that year the Soufriere Hills began to erupt. People had almost forgotten that there was a volcano on the island. Even Grandma (who knows almost everything) had only heard stories about it. No wonder – books say that it had not erupted for over 300 years! But my surprise turned to dismay, as you'll find out in my diary.

18 July
I noticed smoke coming from the top of Chance's Peak in the Soufriere Hills. Our teacher said it was a dormant volcano that had not erupted for centuries. Today it came back to life!

21 July
For the past three days we have felt the ground rumbling. I have never felt an earthquake before. It is quite scary. People living in Long Ground have been **evacuated**.

8 August
The **tremors** from the earthquakes are getting stronger. You can actually feel the buildings move. There is a huge column of ash above the volcano. Grandma was evacuated today to St John's in the north of the island where it is safer.

19 August
It is over a month since the volcano began to erupt. I think it is getting worse. Many people have gone to the north of the island and some people have left Montserrat completely.

21 August
For over half an hour today the sky was dark with ash. The wind blew the ash all over Plymouth. Everything is filthy now.

30 August
The volcano has gone quiet now. Scientists think that there could be a big explosion. My parents say we are going to live in Salem until the volcano quietens down.

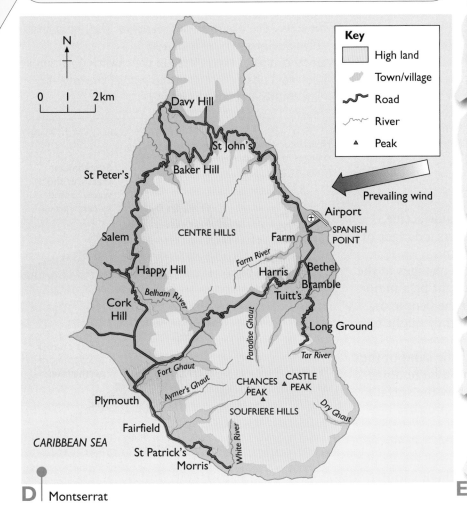

D | Montserrat

E | Extracts from Chander's 1995 diary

Activities

1 Look at map A.
   a) Use an atlas to label a large copy of the map which your teacher will give you.
   b) Find out which other Caribbean island had a major eruption in the twentieth century. When was it? Were people killed?

2 Look at drawing C. It shows how Montserrat and other Caribbean islands were formed.
   a) Write a paragraph to explain how islands were formed in the Caribbean. Use the labels from the drawings as your sentences.

Think about the best order for the sentences so that your paragraph makes sense.
   b) Explain why some Caribbean islands are volcanic and others are not.

3 Read the diary extracts in E.
   a) Locate on map D the places Chander mentions in her diary.
   b) Suggest why Plymouth was in danger. (Use the scale to measure its distance from Chances Peak. Notice the prevailing wind.)
   c) Would St John's be a good place to house people evacuated from Plymouth? Why?

How close can you get?

For many months our family hoped to go back to Plymouth. But every time we thought it might be safe there was another eruption. Eventually at the end of 1996, we decided to leave Montserrat. I was very sad. We had to leave our house and most of our belongings. My parents went back for a day to collect a few valuables. They said that Plymouth was covered in ash.
Now we have moved to Britain. I try to keep in touch with Grandma who is still in St John's. I use the Internet to get all the latest information about the island.

Chander and her cousin, Alena

Even before the Soufriere Hills became active, geologists had warned that there was a danger of an eruption. The Montserrat Volcano Observatory was set up to monitor changes in the volcano and predict when there might be a major eruption. It provided warnings to the people on the island and advised them when they ought to evacuate their homes.

The geologists had noticed that the sides of the volcano had begun to bulge due to a large dome of magma which was growing below the surface. The danger was that the increasing pressure would cause a sudden violent eruption, sending **pyroclastic flows** down the side of the volcano. These are deadly clouds of hot ash and gas moving down slopes and valleys at high speed.

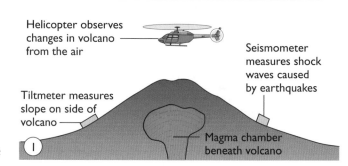

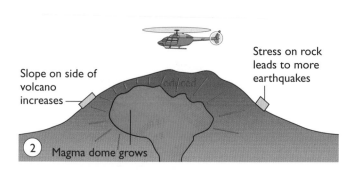

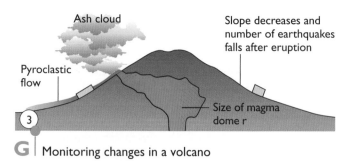

G Monitoring changes in a volcano

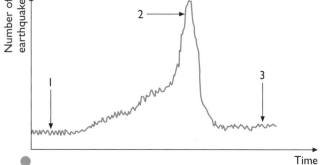

F Seismic recordings during changes in a volcano

Activity
Look at graph F and the drawings in G.
a) Describe three techniques that geologists can use to warn people when a volcano might erupt.
b) Describe the changes that might be observed before an eruption.

Ash all ova de town
You wash all you clothes
An as soon as you turn you back
You clothes, house an everything full up na ash.
You clean you car de Saturday morning,
By afternoon you see ash all under de car.
Now you see wa mec me ha fu come a Britain,
Because de volcano down deya trow out ash all
   ova de town.

H At school in London, Chander wrote a poem about her last memory of Plymouth.

I Soufriere Hills erupting in 1995. Plymouth can be seen in the foreground.

J The death of Plymouth
There was a major eruption of the Soufriere Hills in August 1997. Plymouth was finally destroyed. Tonnes of hot lava and ash poured out of the volcano and set fire to the town. The whole of Plymouth was buried under ash.

Assignment

Where is it safe to live on Montserrat?

You have been asked to divide Montserrat into zones according to the level of danger and mark the zones onto a map of the island. The geologists established the following zones to help the authorities to ensure the safety of people on the island:

- Zone A – too dangerous to enter. Geologists go in by helicopter only
- Zone B – completely evacuated, but people allowed to collect items from their homes
- Zone C – elderly people and children evacuated. Others ready to leave at short notice
- Zone D – safe enough to house people evacuated from other areas.

1 Read the extracts in the box on the right. They are from a report issued by the Montserrat Volcano Observatory on 29 June 1997.

2 On map D on page 13 locate all the places mentioned in the extracts.

3 On a copy of the map that your teacher will give you, divide the islands into zones A, B, C and D.

4 Write a report explaining your reasons for dividing the island into zones in this way.

- The dome on the eastern side of Chances Peak volcano is growing larger.
- Lava, ash and rocks pour down the Tar River valley to the sea producing huge clouds of steam.
- Most vegetation in the south of the island is dead, buried beneath hot ash.
- An ash cloud blown westwards has buried Plymouth beneath centimetres of ash.
- Pyroclastic flows along Paradise Ghaut have reached Harris's village.
- Ash and pebbles fell on Salem causing minor injuries.
- There is a danger of mudflows along many valleys around the Soufriere Hills if it rains.
- A lava flow passed within metres of the school in Cork Hill.
- The airport has been forced to close until further notice.
- A temporary port has been opened at Little Bay near Davy Hill for people to leave the island.

In this Building Block you will find out why San Francisco is threatened by earthquakes and suggest ways to make the city safer.

This will also help you with the USA investigation on page 107.

1.6

Ready for the Big One?

On Tuesday 17 October 1989 an earthquake measuring 7.1 on the Richter scale struck the city of San Francisco in California, USA. Sixty-seven people died. This was not the first earthquake that the city had experienced. In 1906 an earthquake measuring 8.1 virtually destroyed the city, killing 700 people.

A

18 October 1989

STRONG QUAKE HITS SAN FRANCISCO

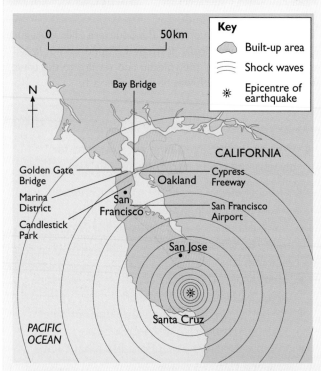

Key

- Built-up area
- Shock waves
- ☀ Epicentre of earthquake

0 — 50 km

N

Bay Bridge

CALIFORNIA

Golden Gate Bridge

Marina District

Candlestick Park

San Francisco

Oakland

Cypress Freeway

San Francisco Airport

San Jose

Santa Cruz

PACIFIC OCEAN

A major earthquake rocked the San Francisco region of California yesterday evening. The epicentre of the quake was about 100 km south-east of the city in the Santa Cruz mountains. At least sixty people are known to have died, with over 3,000 more injured. Thousands of people ran into the streets during the fifteen-second quake, which struck at the start of the evening rush hour at 5.04 p.m.

Motorists were crushed to death when a section of a two-tier motorway – the Cypress Freeway in Oakland – collapsed. The road, which was meant to be earthquake-proof, shook like jelly when the quake hit. More people died at the Bay Bridge when part of the structure collapsed and cars fell into the water below.

At Candlestick Park, the San Francisco baseball stadium, 60,000 fans were packed in to watch an important game. There were screams as the whole stadium swayed for about fifteen seconds, opening up huge cracks. The game was called off and the stadium evacuated. Fortunately, no one here was killed. San Francisco Airport was closed as a result of damage to the runway and buildings. At San Jose, closer to the epicentre, a shopping centre was badly damaged.

One of the worst affected areas of the city was the Marina District. Fires have been burning out of control in an area where many of the houses are built of timber. This area was destroyed by a previous earthquake in 1906.

Damaged homes in the Marina District of the city

San Francisco lies on the San Andreas Fault, a large crack in the Earth's crust that runs down the west coast of the USA. It is part of the boundary between two major plates. To the west the Pacific Plate is sliding northwards past the North American Plate to the east. Movement along the fault is only a few centimetres each year, but in some places the plates become 'locked' together. Tension then builds up within the rock. An earthquake happens when the tension is released with a sudden movement along the fault.

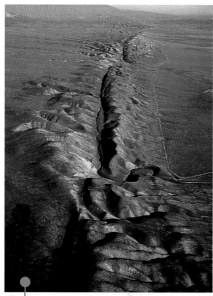

C The San Andreas Fault in California is clearly visible from the air.

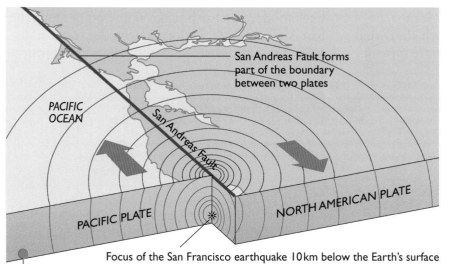

San Andreas Fault forms part of the boundary between two plates

PACIFIC OCEAN

San Andreas Fault

PACIFIC PLATE

NORTH AMERICAN PLATE

Focus of the San Francisco earthquake 10km below the Earth's surface

B Plate movement along the San Andreas Fault

Activities

I Read newspaper extract A. On a large copy of the map write labels to describe what happened at each place mentioned in the article.

2 Look at diagram B.
   a) Explain why San Francisco is in constant danger from earthquakes.
   b) Draw the line of the San Andreas Fault onto your map from activity I.

3 **a)** Look again at source A. From its location, would you have expected the Marina District of the city to be badly damaged? Explain why.
   b) Look at drawing D. Now explain why the Marina District was so badly damaged.
   c) Look at photo E. From the motorway's location, would you have expected this amount of damage? Suggest why it might have happened.

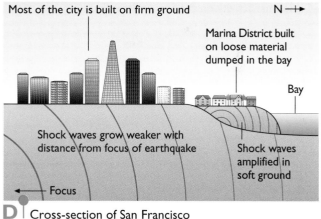

Most of the city is built on firm ground   N →

Marina District built on loose material dumped in the bay

Bay

Shock waves grow weaker with distance from focus of earthquake

Shock waves amplified in soft ground

← Focus

D Cross-section of San Francisco

E The Cypress Freeway collapsed in the earthquake.

BUILDING BLOCKS

How can prediction help?

Geologists use **seismometers** to measure the strength of the shock waves caused by earthquakes. These are so sensitive that they can record even minor tremors that people do not feel. There is probably more recording equipment along the San Andreas Fault than along any other fault in the world.

The amount of **seismic activity**, or number of earthquakes, varies along the fault. Some stretches have frequent shocks, which show that the plates on either side of the fault are moving.

But there are also **seismic gaps** along the fault, where there are few earthquakes. In these places the plates are locked together and tension is building up in the rocks, making a major earthquake more likely. This happened on the Loma Prieta Gap before the earthquake in 1989.

Geologists can now forecast the probability, or likelihood, of an earthquake at any point along the San Andreas Fault. Unfortunately, they cannot predict exactly when an earthquake will happen.

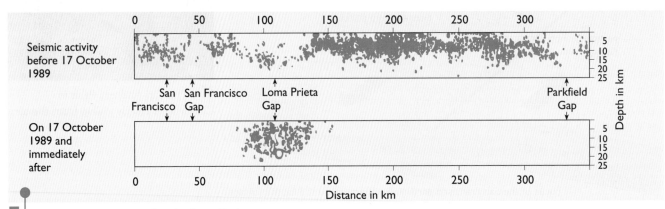

F Seismic activity on the San Andreas Fault

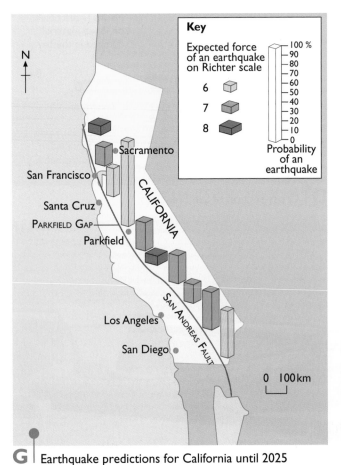

G Earthquake predictions for California until 2025

Activities

1 Look at the graphs in box F.
  a) Describe the distribution of seismic activity shown in the first graph. Mention at what depth most earthquakes occur; the points along the fault where they mostly happen; where the seismic gaps are.
  b) Describe the distribution of seismic activity in the second graph, after the 1989 earthquake.
  c) Explain why the earthquake happened.

2 Look at map G.
  a) Where is the most likely place for the next earthquake?
  b) What (as a percentage) is the probability of an earthquake there?
  c) How strong is it likely to be (on the Richter scale)?
  d) Where is the most powerful earthquake likely to be?
  e) How strong will it be?
  f) What is the probability of this happening?
  g) What is the probability of an earthquake in San Francisco itself? How would you feel if you were living there?

Assignment

Plan an earthquake-proof San Francisco

The California State Government wants to reduce the damage caused by future earthquakes in San Francisco. New buildings and roads must be earthquake-proof and old ones need to be strengthened. Vital buildings, such as schools and hospitals, should be in the safest areas, while the most dangerous areas should be reserved for parks and open space.

I Your teacher will give you a large copy of map I and map J. Look at map I, which shows the seismic hazard, or danger from earthquakes, in each part of San Francisco. Seismic hazard is worked out from the type of rock in each part of the city and the distance from the San Andreas Fault.

2 Look at map J. It shows the main roads and public buildings in the city.

   Trace your copy of this map to place over the seismic hazard map. Where seismic hazard is high roads and buildings need to be strengthened. They should not be built at all where the hazard is greatest. Identify the sections of road and the major buildings that need to be strengthened. Highlight them on your map.

3 Choose a suitable location for each of the following and mark them on your map.

H | The Transamerica Pyramid in the city centre of San Francisco was built to withstand earthquakes. It is said to be able to sway up to 12 metres without collapse.

- a new hospital
- a new waterside residential area
- a new park
- a route for a new railway linking the city centre to Candlestick Park.

4 Write a short report to explain your decisions.

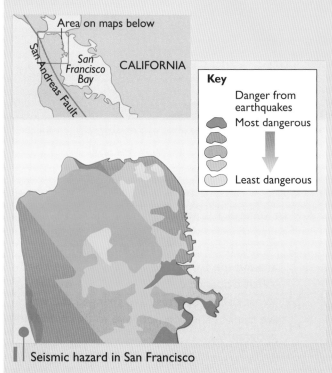

I | Seismic hazard in San Francisco

Key

Danger from earthquakes

Most dangerous

Least dangerous

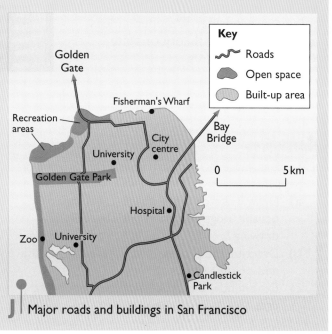

J | Major roads and buildings in San Francisco

Key

~ Roads

Open space

Built-up area

DIGGING DEEPER

1.7 What on earth has happened?

A | Alfred Wegener

It is hard to imagine that the earth beneath your feet is actually moving. Yet geologists now believe that this is happening all around the world. According to the theory of **plate tectonics**, the large plates that form the Earth's crust are constantly moving (see map H on page 10).

This idea was first suggested by the scientist Alfred Wegener in 1923. He said that all the world's continents were once joined together in one large super-continent, that he called 'Pangaea'. About 250 million years ago this split into separate continents that have been moving slowly, or drifting, ever since. This process is called **continental drift**. At the time he put forward this idea few people believed Wegener. Geological evidence suggested the continents might have once been joined, but nobody could believe that rocks moved!

For many years after Wegener's death his ideas were almost forgotten. However, the development of submarines during the Second World War enabled geologists to get a much clearer picture of the ocean floor than they had before. And what they saw surprised them.

Running down the middle of the world's oceans are long mountain chains, or **mid-oceanic ridges**. Where the ridges rise above the surface of the ocean volcanic islands are formed. In fact, all along each ridge there is evidence that volcanic activity is forming new rock or mountains under the sea. As this happens it pushes the older rocks on either side of the ridge further apart, making the ocean wider. It was this discovery that made geologists reconsider Wegener's ideas and to propose the theory of plate tectonics in the 1960s.

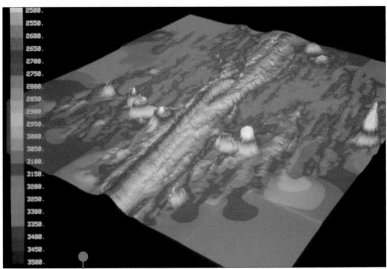

B | A computer-simulated image of a mid-oceanic ridge. The scale shows metres below sea level.

Activities

1 Look at image B. Compare it with the drawing on page 11.
   a) Draw a sketch of the image. Label the mid-oceanic ridge and plates with the help of drawing I.
   b) Describe the process that is happening at the mid-oceanic ridge.
   c) Explain how this process causes continental drift.

2 Plate tectonics is not the only theory to have changed the way we think.
   a) People once believed that the Sun moved around the Earth. What do we believe now? What evidence could you use to prove it?
   b) What other theories have changed the way we think? (They do not have to be to do with geography.)

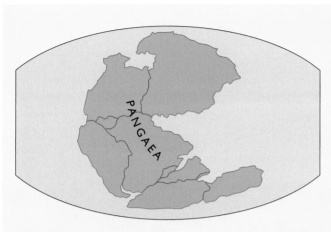

250 million years ago the continents were joined together in one huge land mass called Pangaea

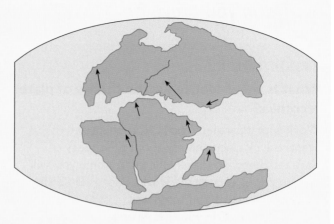

180 million years ago Pangaea had begun to break up, forming two smaller continents

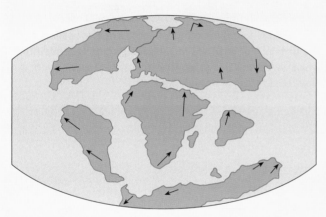

70 million years ago the shape of today's continents had become clearer

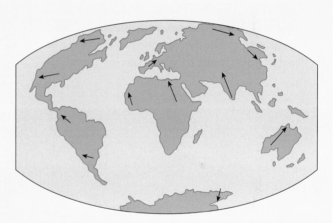

The world today

Continental drift

3 Look at the world maps in box C.
  a) Describe carefully the main changes that you can see that happened between each pair of maps:
      i)   250 million to 180 million years ago
      ii) 180 million to 70 million years ago
      iii) 70 million years ago to the present day.
  b) Suggest what changes might happen over the next 100 million years. (The arrows showing the direction in which continents are moving will give you clues.)
  c) Draw a sketch map to show what the world might look like 100 million years from now.

Homework

4 a) Trace the outline of the world's continents as they are today from a world map. Cut the shapes out.
  b) Place the shapes on a sheet of paper and see how well you can get them to fit together. When you have done it, stick the shapes down. Give the new map a title.

5 a) Think about what you have studied on this page. What evidence do we have that plate tectonics theory is true?
  b) Suggest at least two other pieces of evidence that you might want as proof of this theory.

DIGGING DEEPER

How can you prove it?

Assignment

What is the evidence for the theory of plate tectonics?

Work with a partner. You have been invited to prepare a TV documentary about the theory of plate tectonics. To make your programme you will have to travel all over the world. Photos D–G show some of the places you could visit.

For each location you visit write a short script to explain how evidence there helps to prove the theory of plate tectonics.

Think about what you have learnt about earthquakes, volcanoes and plate tectonics in this unit and look back to check your ideas. You could start your script with the sentences under the photos.

Present your script to your class.

D Coal is found in countries that have a cool climate, like Britain. Yet coal was formed under tropical conditions when vegetation in swamp forests died and was buried. How could this have happened?

E Ascension Island in the middle of the Atlantic Ocean is one of many volcanic islands in the middle of oceans. But how did they get there?

F The prehistoric reptile, Mesosaurus, has been found as a fossil in rocks in both southern Africa and South America. Why is it found in both places?

G Dwyka tillite, a rock found in South Africa (a warm country), was formed by frozen glaciers. Identical rock is found in Brazil and India (not very cold countries!), as well as in Antarctica. How can it be found in such different places, so far apart?

Here I am standing in a coal mine in Yorkshire, England. This ordinary coal supports an extraordinary theory – that the Earth is on the move. Let me explain …

Housing in Rio de Janeiro, Brazil

Development means changes for the better. As a country develops, so the quality of life of the people there improves. There are differences in quality of life between countries and also within countries. Here you can see how quality of life can vary within a city.

- In which of the two living areas in the photo do you think people would have a better quality of life?
- What three words would you use to describe the shanty housing and what three words would you use to describe the apartment housing?
- Where would you rather live? Why?
- From the evidence in the photo, how does quality of life in Rio de Janeiro compare to the UK?

GROUNDWORK

2.1 **W**hat is the quality of life in your area?

Some parts of the UK are more developed than other parts. Wherever you look you will see examples of development: new shopping centres, housing projects, school improvements, airport extensions ... even a dome! But each place is developing at its own rate. There are different levels of development within British cities just as in Rio de Janeiro (see page 23). These differences can be investigated by comparing the quality of life for people in different areas.

A New homes being built – an example of development

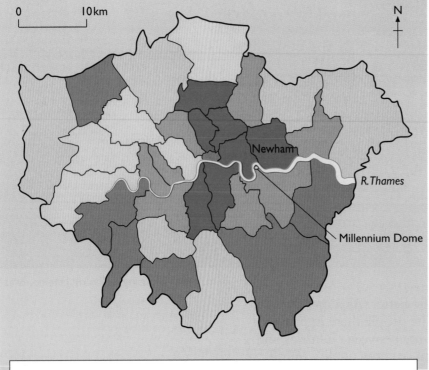

Key

Quality of life compared to national average

Worse than average:
- Over 32% worse
- 25–32% worse
- Up to 25% worse

Better than average:
- Up to 13% better
- Over 13% better

B Quality of life in each London borough compared with the rest of England. Quality of life is measured by combining data on things like health, education and wealth.

Source: *London Facts and Figures*, Office for National Statistics © Crown copyright 2000

Activities

1 Work with a partner.
   a) Think about what is necessary for a good quality of life. Make a list of your ideas.
   b) Compare your ideas with another pair. How many of your ideas are the same? Agree a list of ten ideas and rank them in order of importance.
   c) Look at photos A and C. Explain how each development project could improve the quality of life for people in that area.

2 Look at map B.
   a) Describe the pattern of quality of life in London.
   b) How does the quality of life in different parts of London compare to the rest of the country?

C | The Millennium Dome in London, seen from Canning Town

The Millennium Dome (photo C) was built to celebrate the year 2000 – the beginning of the new millennium. It cost about £750 million to build. It is surrounded by areas of London where the quality of life is among the poorest in the UK. Residents of Canning Town, an area in Newham that overlooks the Dome on the opposite bank of the River Thames, were asked about their priorities for improving their quality of life.

There is a lot of crime in this area. Car crime is the worst. Every day you see vandalised cars. Companies charge the earth to insure cars around here, so people can't afford to have them. We need to have more policing.

I'd like to see better buildings in the area. Most of the schools are falling apart and that doesn't make a good environment to learn in. Lots of people live in tower blocks and they're not safe.

Pollution is terrible. The A13 goes right through the middle of Canning Town and it's one of the busiest roads into London. Many children suffer from asthma – a lot more than the national average. They should ban cars and have better public transport.

3 Read source D.
  a) What are the residents' priorities for improving quality of life in Canning Town?
  b) Suggest what views they might have about the Millennium Dome that has been built close by. What benefits or problems might it bring?

D | Views of residents in Canning Town
Source: Mayflower Family Centre

Local investigation

What is the quality of life in your local area?
Carry out an investigation to find out people's views.

1 In small groups, design a questionnaire to find out what people think about quality of life in your local area and what their priorities are for improving it.

Consider including multiple-choice or yes–no questions in your questionnaire, as these will give you results that are easier to work with. A few carefully chosen questions will probably produce better results.

2 Carry out a survey using the questionnaire. *Either* interview people that you know *or*, working as a group, interview people in the local high street.

You could also take photos or a video film to use when presenting your findings.

3 Share your results with the rest of the class. Organise your results to show your findings. A database programme may help you to present the results using graphs, maps and diagrams.

4 Write up your investigation. You could send a copy to local politicians who have to make decisions about the future of the area.

FRAMEWORK

2.2 **W**hat is development?

Geographers distinguish between **more economically developed countries (MEDCs)** and **less economically developed countries (LEDCs)**, sometimes called developing countries, underdeveloped countries or the 'Third World'.

They often measure the level of development in a country by its wealth per person, or **gross national product per capita** (GNP/capita). This is calculated by dividing **gross national product (GNP)** by the country's population. Poor countries, with a low GNP/capita, are said to be less economically developed. Rich countries, with a high GNP/capita, are said to be more economically developed.

But is it really helpful to divide the world this way? **Economic growth,** or increase in a country's wealth, may not be the best way of measuring development. A country may produce increasing quantities of goods and earn more money without there being an improvement in people's quality of life. Wealth might not be shared, so only a few people in the country might benefit. Economic growth can also bring its own problems which actually harm quality of life, such as environmental pollution and crime.

However, despite these problems, wealth is still widely used as a measure of the level of development in each country.

Development

Growth

A Development and growth

B Homelessness in the UK, an MEDC

Country	GNP (US $ million)	Population (million)	GNP/capita
France	1,533,600	58	26,441
India	357,800	945	
South Africa	132,500	38	
USA	7,433,500	265	
UK	1,152,100	59	

C GNP and population for five countries. GNP is given in US dollars so countries can be compared.
Source: World Bank 1998

D Education in Eritrea, an LEDC

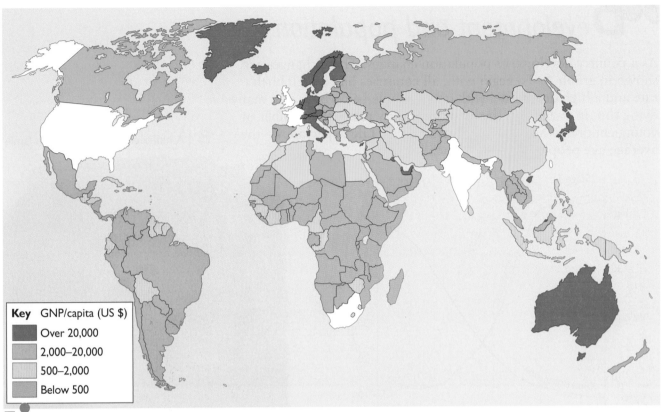

E GNP/capita around the world. The five countries in table C are blank here.

Key GNP/capita (US $)
- Over 20,000
- 2,000–20,000
- 500–2,000
- Below 500

Activities

1 Look at cartoon A.
- **a)** Describe the message of the cartoon.
- **b)** Use the cartoon to explain the difference between development and economic growth in a country.

2 Study table C.
- **a)** For each country in the table, work out the GNP/capita. For each country, divide the GNP by the population. One has been done for you. Complete a copy of the table.
- **b)** Explain why India, with a higher GNP than South Africa, is actually a poorer country.

3 Look at photos B and D.
- **a)** What do the photos tell you about the quality of life for some people in these countries?
- **b)** Use the photos to help you explain that economic growth and development are not always the same.

4 Look at map E.
- **a)** Use the information in table C to help you to complete a copy of the map. Shade each country on the map to show its GNP/capita.

- **b)** Some people refer to the rich and poor parts of the world as the 'North' and the 'South'. On your map, try to draw a line to divide the world into the 'rich North' and the 'poor South'. The line should go from east to west on the map, but can bend as much as you want.
- **c)** Is it helpful to divide the world in this way? Give reasons for your answer.

5 a) In what ways do you think GNP/capita is a good measure of development? In what ways is it not a good measure?
- **b)** Suggest other things that you could use to measure development. You could include some of your ideas from activity 1 on page 24.

Homework

6 Find two newspaper stories, one about an MEDC and the other about an LEDC. Cut them out and stick them in your workbook.

For each story, explain what it tells you about the level of development in that country.

2.3 Development and population

As a country develops, its population changes. These changes are shown in graph A. To begin with, all countries had a high **birth rate** and a high **death rate**, with many people being born and many dying too. In particular, the **infant mortality rate** – the number of young children who die – was much higher. **Life expectancy** – the average age people died – was much lower.

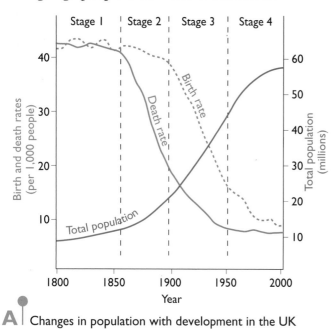

A | Changes in population with development in the UK

B | A nineteenth-century British family

Activities

1 Compare photos B and C.

a) Describe what the photos tell you about changes in the quality of life in Britain since the nineteenth century.

b) Suggest why families in nineteenth-century Britain were larger than they are today.

2 Look at graph A, which is divided into four stages.

a) Choose the correct title to describe each stage:

- low death rate, falling birth rate
- high death rate and high birth rate
- low death rate and low birth rate
- falling death rate, high birth rate.

Write the titles on a large copy of the graph.

b) Describe the changes in death rate and birth rate that happen as a country develops.

c) Describe the changes that happen to the total population as a country develops. Use the changes in birth rate and death rate to explain the changes in the total population.

3 a) Read the details below about several generations of the same family. Label your graph to show when each person was born and show their lifespan with a horizontal line.

Benjamin Blake	1880–1915. Son of Hannah. Railway worker until First World War. Died in France.
Jake Perkins	Born 1980. Only son of Jane.
Josiah Smith	1782–1830. Farmworker in Devon. Father of six children.
Peter Perkins	Born 1929. Son of Dorothy. Engineer with London Transport. Two children.
Rebecca Smith	1821–26. Youngest daughter of Josiah. Died of typhoid.
Jane Perkins	Born 1956. First member of family to go to university. A lawyer with one child.
Hannah Blake	1841–1906. Granddaughter of Josiah. Domestic servant in Bath. Mother of eight children (five died as young children).
Dora Perkins	1901–70. Only child of Benjamin. Moved to London. Mother of four children.

As a country develops, first the death rate falls, leading to **natural increase** in the population. Later, the birth rate also falls, until birth and death rates both reach a low level so natural increase slows down. By this time infant mortality is low and life expectancy is high.

The population of any country at a particular time can be shown by a graph called a **population pyramid**. This shows how the population is made up, by gender and age group. Graphs D and E show the population of the UK in 1871 and 1991.

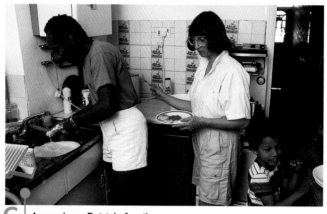

C A modern British family

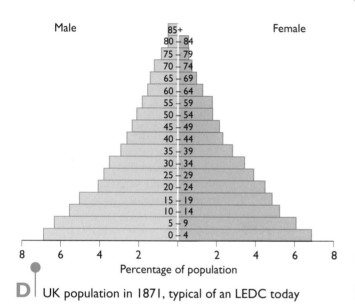

D UK population in 1871, typical of an LEDC today

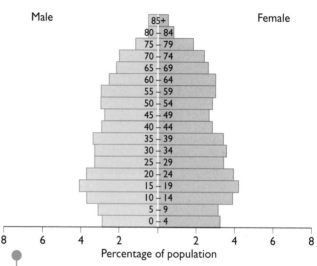

E UK population in 1991, typical of an MEDC today

b) Describe the changes in infant mortality and life expectancy that happen as a country develops. Use evidence from the family on your graph to help you.

4 Look at population pyramids D and E.
  a) Sketch the outline shape of each pyramid. Give each sketch a title.
  b) Choose three labels for each pyramid from the box below. Write the labels on the correct part of each pyramid sketch.

> sloping sides show high natural increase
> wide top shows low death rate
> wide base shows high birth rate
> narrow top shows high death rate
> vertical sides show low natural increase
> narrow base shows low birth rate

c) Use the two pyramids to compare the population of an MEDC and an LEDC.

5 Look at the data in table F.
  a) For each country in the table, suggest which stage in graph A it has reached. Give reasons in each case.
  b) For each country, draw a sketch to show how its population pyramid might look.

Country	Birth rate	Death rate	Infant mortality	Life expectancy
France	13	9	5	78
India	25	9	65	63
USA	15	8	7	77
Zambia	43	18	112	45

F Population data for four countries in 1999

2.4 Trade and aid

Throughout history, countries have traded with each other. A country that produces certain goods is able to **trade** them for things produced by other countries that it needs. Trade like this benefits both countries. In this way countries have become **interdependent** – relying on each other for many of the goods they need.

Over the past few centuries the countries of Europe and other more economically developed countries have come to dominate world trade. Trade now benefits some countries more than others.

Hundreds of years ago people in each part of the world had their own traditional way of life. Often they traded with the countries around them.

From the fifteenth century European explorers arrived in Africa, Asia and America, often with guns. They took gold, silver and other valuable goods, such as spices, often paying nothing in exchange.

The Europeans conquered the people and **colonised** their land. Millions of African people were taken to America to work as slaves.

Land was used to produce **primary goods,** such as tea, coffee, sugar and cotton. These primary goods were sent by ship to supply factories in Europe.

Using these **imported** cheap **raw materials** they were able to produce **manufactured goods,** such as textiles from cotton.

Europe **exported** its manufactured goods around the world and became richer. The history of colonisation and unequal trade is one of the main reasons that some countries are more economically developed than others today.

A A brief history of trade

B Countries like the Philippines still depend on exporting primary goods.

C The pattern of world trade

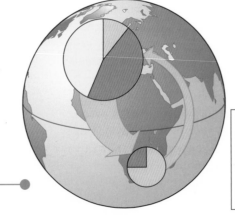

Key

	Primary goods
	Manufactured goods
	Services

Today, MEDCs can help to improve the quality of life of people in LEDCs by providing **aid**. In practice, however, most MEDCs spend only a tiny fraction of their money on aid – in the UK aid is just 0.3 per cent of government spending.

Aid is given in two main ways:

- **Short-term aid** is given during or immediately after disasters such as earthquakes, floods or wars. It brings help quickly to people affected by the disaster.
- **Long-term aid** is given to enable countries to develop and to improve people's quality of life over time.

Countries giving aid do not always understand the problems faced by LEDCs, and the aid they give may not be appropriate. For example, some aid projects are too big and cost too much money to run. Large projects, such as dams designed to control flooding or produce electricity, can damage the natural environment and also destroy people's traditional way of life. Aid projects may ignore local people's knowledge and skills, and may not provide any jobs for local people. Sometimes the aid does not even reach the people it was meant to help, because of poor transport, war or a corrupt government that keeps the money for itself.

The best aid projects usually involve appropriate aid – aid that is suited to the country in which it is to be used, that makes use of local people's knowledge and skills and that does not destroy the environment or traditional lifestyles.

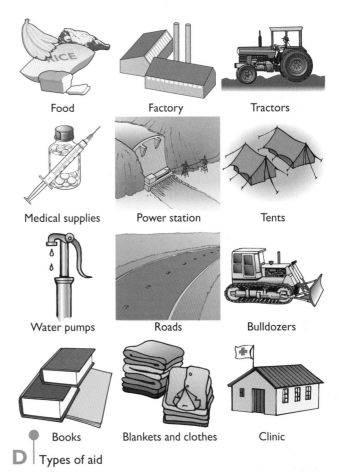

Food   Factory   Tractors

Medical supplies   Power station   Tents

Water pumps   Roads   Bulldozers

Books   Blankets and clothes   Clinic

D   Types of aid

E   This clinic in Jessore, Bangladesh was built with aid money. Here a Bangladeshi health worker is teaching rural women about food hygiene and nutrition.

Activities

1 **a)** From source A, describe at least three ways in which you think that people in Europe treated people in other parts of the world unfairly.
   b) Rewrite the story as it might have happened if people had treated each other fairly. What differences might this have made to the world today?

2 Look at photo B and diagram C.
   a) Describe what the diagram shows you.
   b) Explain how this pattern helps to keep LEDCs poor and MEDCs rich.

3 Look at box D.
   a) List the types of aid under two headings: short-term aid and long-term aid.
   b) Suggest four types of aid that might be useful to a country:
   i) after an earthquake
   ii) to improve the quality of life in a rural area.
   Give reasons for each item you include.

4 Look at photo E.
   a) Do you think this is appropriate aid? Give reasons.
   b) Write six rules that MEDCs should follow when giving aid to poorer countries.

In this Building Block you will compare ideas about development from people in the USA and Zambia. You will then use your own ideas to compare levels of development in ten countries.
This will also help you with the USA investigation on page 107.

2.5 **W**hat does development mean to you?

The United States of America is one of the richest countries in the world. It is an MEDC. We asked some pupils at a school near Chicago what they understood by the word 'development', and how they saw the USA.

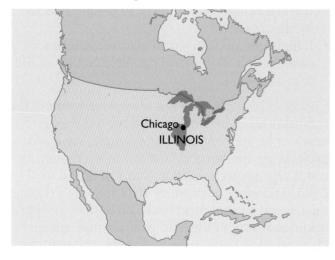

> I'm proud to live in America. We have lots of freedom here that you don't get elsewhere. You can say what you want and be who you want – that's really important. I don't think development is just about wealth. In the USA we often put possessions before our families. But in countries where people suffer because they are poor, families are real close. I wish we had that.

> The USA is still developing. The population is growing because people keep coming here for opportunities. It's got a lot to do with money because here we have the technology to build skyscrapers and make the latest computers. But there is a problem here with education. They reckon that kids in Japan and China do much better than us. Too many kids here don't pass their grades and that is going to hold the country back.

A Maria, Adam and Jaime, pupils at Joliet Central High School near Chicago in Illinois. Education here, as in most schools in the USA, is free.

> America is a melting pot with lots of different races and cultures, but often you find that whites live in one area while blacks and Hispanics live in others. Crime is a big issue. Too many people abuse the freedom we have by stealing, or worse. The government needs to make punishments tougher for them. And they should spend more money to sort out problems here rather than getting involved with other people's problems around the world.

B A residential area in Joliet

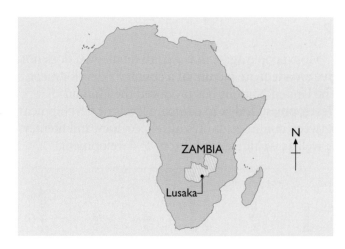

Zambia, in Africa, is one of the world's poorest countries. It is an LEDC. We asked some pupils at a school in Lusaka, the capital city, what they understood by the word 'development' and how they saw Zambia.

We have a beautiful country. Zambia is rich in natural resources, like mineral reserves, water and wildlife, but we don't have advanced technology to exploit them. Zambia has been independent since 1964, but progress has been very slow. Zimbabwe (Zambia's neighbour) achieved independence after Zambia, but it is more developed. Their road network and transport system are better than ours.

I don't think Zambia is very developed. Many people are very sick and there are not enough hospitals. Many children cannot read, and there are not enough schools. At the same time, government ministers drive around in expensive cars. This means that the government is spending money, but not on things that people need. I am happy with the school that I go to and think that I am very lucky, as many people don't have that opportunity.

Development should involve equality too. There is no equality for the African girl. In a family, the guy will go to school and the girl is expected to help in the kitchen and to grow up to be a good wife. I'm very lucky that my parents don't think in this way. They think men and women should co-operate with each other. We should end the custom of having so many children to demonstrate wealth. People have to learn to use contraception to space their children, in order to care for the ones they have.

C Salma, Tendai and Tamara, pupils at St Mary's Convent School in Lusaka. Pupils here have to pay for their education.

Activities

1 Read all the ideas about development on these two pages.
   a) In two columns, one for each country, summarise the main ideas about development that the pupils mention.
   b) How are people's ideas about development influenced by the country in which they live? Give examples to support your answer.

2 Work in a small group. Discuss these questions:
   a) What do *you* think 'development' is about?
   b) i) In what ways do you think the UK is more developed?
      ii) In what ways do you think the UK is less developed?
   Write down your ideas to help you with the assignment on page 35.

D A residential area in Lusaka

How would you measure development?

The USA and Zambia are two countries where the quality of life, or level of development, is widely different. But how could you *measure* this? Things that are used to measure development are called development indicators.

Most people agree that wealth on its own does not give an adequate picture of a country's development. The United Nations has produced the **Human Development Index** to compare levels of development between countries. It uses life expectancy and literacy, as well as wealth, as indicators of development.

DEVELOPMENT INDICATORS		Brazil	China	France	India	Japan	Nigeria	Russian Federation	UK	USA	Zambia
	GNP/capita (US $)	4,400	750	26,270	380	40,940	240	2,410	19,600	28,020	360
	Life expectancy (years)	67	69	78	63	80	53	67	77	77	45
	% of people with access to safe water	72	90	100	81	–	39	–	100	90	43
	Population growth (%)	1.8	1.3	0.5	2.0	0.5	3.0	0.4	0.3	1.0	3.0
	Energy consumption (kg oil/capita)	772	707	4,150	260	3,964	165	4,079	3,786	7,905	145
	Urban population (%)	79	31	75	27	78	40	76	89	76	43
	People per doctor	847	642	333	2,439	613	5,882	215	623	408	11,111
	Infant mortality (per 1,000 births)	36	33	5	65	4	78	17	6	7	112
	Adult literacy (%)	83	81	99	51	99	57	99	99	99	78
	% workforce employed in agriculture	23	72	5	64	7	43	14	2	3	75
	% children aged 5–11 in primary school	90	99	99	93	100	–	100	100	96	77
	Cars (per 1,000 people)	79	8	524	7	552	12	158	399	767	26

E Development indicators for ten countries (– = no figures available)

Sources: World Bank 1998, UNDP 1996

F

Activities

1 Look at the countries in table E and map G.
List the countries in order from the one that you think is most developed down to the least developed. Keep your list until you have completed the assignment on page 35.

2 Look at photos F and H.
a) i) What do they show about quality of life and development?
ii) Why are these difficult to measure?
b) List other indicators of development that are difficult to measure. Can you suggest ways to measure any of them?

1 Brazil	6 Nigeria
2 China	7 Russian Federation
3 France	8 UK
4 India	9 USA
5 Japan	10 Zambia

G Location of ten countries

H

Assignment

How will you measure development?

 You are going to complete your own Development Index to compare levels of development in ten countries. You could use a spreadsheet package on a computer.

1 **a)** Choose the six indicators of development from table E that you think are the most important.

 b) Rank the six indicators in order of importance. Write them in order on a large copy of the table on the right, in the spaces across the top. Write the names of the countries in the left-hand column.

2 **a)** In table E, find data for your six indicators for each country.

 b) Give each country a score from 1 to 10 for each indicator.

 Give 10 points to the country with the highest level of development for this indicator, down to 1 point to the country with the lowest level.

 For example, if you chose life expectancy, Japan would score 10 points and Zambia 1 point. The UK and the USA would both score 8 points, and you would miss out the next rank score (7 points).

 Write the scores in your table.

 c) For each score you give, multiply it by the number at the top of the next column to get a weighted score. For example, all the scores in the first column should be multiplied by 6. Write the weighted scores in the second column.

Country	x6	x5	x4	x3	x2	x1	Development index

3 Work out a total score for each country by adding the six weighted scores. Write these in the final column. This is your Development Index. Rank the countries according to their level of development.

4 Look at the rank order in your table.
 a) Compare the order with your list from activity 1. Is the rank order the same? Which countries are most developed and which are least developed?
 b) i) Where does the UK appear in your rank order?
 ii) Look back at what you wrote for activity 2 on page 33. Have any of your ideas changed?

In this Building Block you will play Developmania to find out how some countries were able to develop more than others.

2.6

Why did some countries develop more than others?

Have you played the game Monopoly? Developmania is rather like it. But in this game you buy countries rather than streets, and you don't charge rent, you sell products. In both games – as in the real world – there are losers as well as winners.

Activities

Play Developmania in a group of four. One person will need to take the role of banker in the game.
    To play the game you will need:

- a token for each player and a dice
- money, 'Boom or Bust' cards and factories, which your teacher will give you.

How to play

1   Each player chooses a European country. There is one on each corner of the game. Place your token on your home square (your token could be a small flag). Each player starts the game with $20,000 from the bank. Collect $2,000 every time you pass your home square.

2   Take turns to roll the dice. Move your token clockwise, counting the number of squares shown on the dice. If you roll a six, pick up a 'Boom or Bust' card. Follow the instructions on the card and then place it face down at the bottom of the pile.

3   Each time you land on a country or a company you have the option to buy it, if it is not already owned. Pay the price on the square to the bank. You are also allowed to buy countries or companies from other players, and to do swaps.

4   Each time you land on a **country** that is already owned, you have to pay for the products that it produces. The amount you pay depends on the products – see the prices on the table in the centre of the gameboard. For example, if you land on Jamaica, you must pay $400 ($200 for sugar, $200 for bananas). Pay the money to the owner.

5   Each time you land on a **company** that is already owned, pay the owner 100 times the number you threw on the dice. But: if the owner owns two companies, you pay 200 times; three companies pay 300 times; four companies pay 400 times.

6   If you own two countries that produce the same product (e.g. India and Brazil both produce cotton) you can build a factory in your own country. Pay $5,000 to the bank for a factory. Write a label on the factory to show what it produces. Each time a player lands on your home square they now have to pay for the manufactured product, which is five times the price of the primary product.

7   Play the game until one player has taken over the world, or until the time allowed by your teacher is over. Add the value of each player's countries, factories and money to find out who is the winner.

Assignment

Why did some countries develop more than others?

Use your experience of the Developmania game to answer this question.

1   Choose two countries from the game, one MEDC, such as the UK, and one LEDC, such as India. Write a paragraph about each country, describing what happened to them in the game.

2   Carry out some research to find out more about the two countries. You could use a CD-ROM encyclopedia.

- What happened to each country in real life?
- Did it rule over an empire or was it ruled by others?
- What primary goods and what manufactured goods does it produce?
- How might this affect its development?
- What is the quality of life like in each country today?

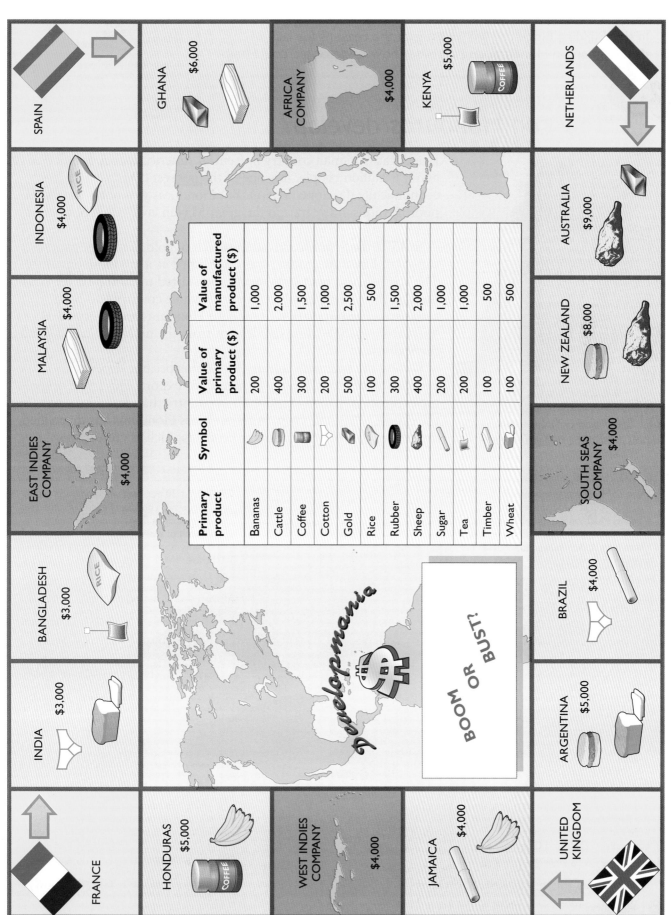

Primary product	Symbol	Value of primary product ($)	Value of manufactured product ($)
Bananas		200	1,000
Cattle		400	2,000
Coffee		300	1,500
Cotton		200	1,000
Gold		500	2,500
Rice		100	500
Rubber		300	1,500
Sheep		400	2,000
Sugar		200	1,000
Tea		200	1,000
Timber		100	500
Wheat		100	500

SPAIN

GHANA $6,000

AFRICA COMPANY $4,000

KENYA $5,000

NETHERLANDS

INDONESIA $4,000

MALAYSIA $4,000

EAST INDIES COMPANY $4,000

BANGLADESH $3,000

INDIA $3,000

FRANCE

HONDURAS $5,000

WEST INDIES COMPANY $4,000

JAMAICA $4,000

UNITED KINGDOM

ARGENTINA $5,000

BRAZIL $4,000

SOUTH SEAS COMPANY $4,000

NEW ZEALAND $8,000

AUSTRALIA $9,000

Developmania

BOOM OR BUST?

BUILDING BLOCKS

In this Building Block you will investigate the reasons for lack of development in Honduras and consider how trade or aid could help.

2.1

How can Honduras develop?

A | The Mayan civilisation built impressive cities 1,000 years ago.

Honduras is a small country in Central America with a population of about 6 million people. It is one of the poorest countries in a less economically developed region. But Honduras was not always so poor. A thousand years ago the great Mayan civilisation flourished there.

In 1502 the Spanish arrived in search of gold. Tegucigalpa, the capital of Honduras today, was established as a gold-mining centre. The Spanish also built settlements and started to farm near the coast, until by the mid-sixteenth century the whole country had been colonised. The population of modern Honduras are described as 'mestizos' – people of mixed descent from the native Americans and the Spanish.

During the twentieth century Honduras became dependent on the production of crops, mainly bananas, for export. This is the origin of the expression 'banana republic' – a country that depends heavily on the export of a single crop. In recent years Honduras has diversified into the export of other primary products, such as coffee.

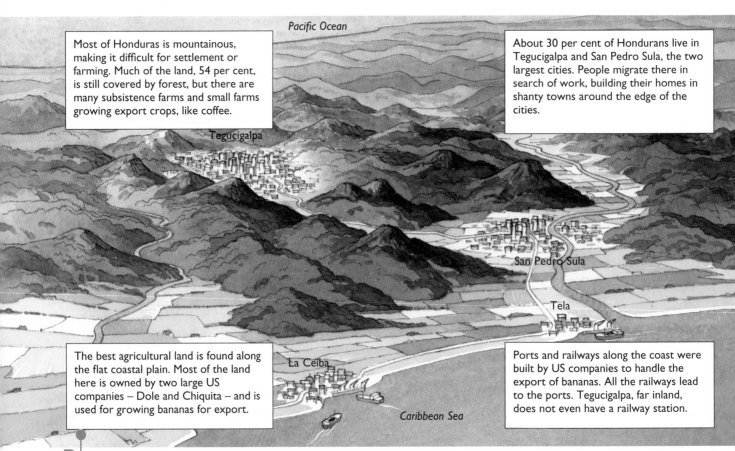

Pacific Ocean

Most of Honduras is mountainous, making it difficult for settlement or farming. Much of the land, 54 per cent, is still covered by forest, but there are many subsistence farms and small farms growing export crops, like coffee.

Tegucigalpa

About 30 per cent of Hondurans live in Tegucigalpa and San Pedro Sula, the two largest cities. People migrate there in search of work, building their homes in shanty towns around the edge of the cities.

San Pedro Sula

Tela

The best agricultural land is found along the flat coastal plain. Most of the land here is owned by two large US companies – Dole and Chiquita – and is used for growing bananas for export.

La Ceiba

Caribbean Sea

Ports and railways along the coast were built by US companies to handle the export of bananas. All the railways lead to the ports. Tegucigalpa, far inland, does not even have a railway station.

B | Honduras

I work for an American company on a huge banana plantation. They employ hundreds of workers on low wages. We only receive a small fraction of the money that people in Europe and America pay for bananas. My family used to own a small farm but it was hard to survive. So they sold the land to a company and now I have to work to survive.

Like other LEDCs, Honduras depends on a few primary products for most of its income. The problem with this is that if crops fail or if prices go down, the country receives less money. The world prices for primary products fluctuate depending on how much people are prepared to pay for them. Over many years the trend is for the price of most primary products to fall, which is bad news for countries like Honduras.

C A worker on a US-owned banana plantation

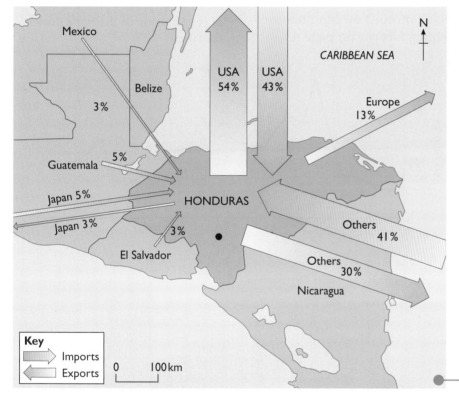

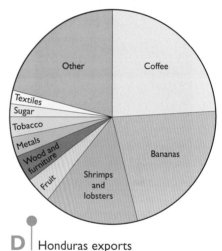

D Honduras exports

E Honduras imports and exports

Activities

1 Look at drawing B.
   a) Describe the location of the largest cities in Honduras: Tegucigalpa, San Pedro Sula and La Ceiba.
   b) Explain the location of each city from the country's history of colonisation.
   c) Which city has the most difficult location for modern needs? Give reasons.

2 Look at sources B, C and E.
   a) Describe the impact of the US influence in Honduras today.

   b) Suggest advantages and disadvantages that this influence might have for people in Honduras.

3 Look at graph D and map E.
   a) Produce two tables to show:
      i) where Honduras' imports and exports come from and go to
      ii) the goods that Honduras exports.
   b) Explain what problems Honduras might face as a result of the pattern of trade shown in your tables.

Fair trade or more aid?

Honduras, like many LEDCs, has to struggle just to maintain people's quality of life. Since 1980 development has slowed down and, for some, the quality of life has deteriorated.

One of the main problems is that Honduras owes a huge amount of **international debt**. Honduras' total debt is greater than its GNP for a whole year. In 1998 it repaid $564 million of debt – almost $100 for every man, woman and child in the country. But the country's debt is still enormous.

In order to solve the problem of debt, many LEDCs increase their production of crops and other primary products for export. As other countries do the same, surplus products on the world market cause prices to fall. As a result, there is a cycle of debt and poverty where countries like Honduras earn less money from exports even though they are producing more. You can find out more about international debt in Digging Deeper on page 43.

F A banana plantation in Honduras. As for other primary products, the price of bananas on the world market has fallen.

Growers 10%

Exporters 10%

COFFEE

Shippers and roasters 55%

Retailers 25%

G Where the money paid for an average jar of coffee goes
Source: Oxfam

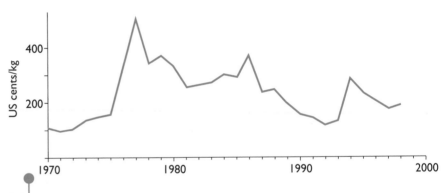

H The price of coffee received by growers
Source: International Coffee Organisation

One way for people in MEDCs to help LEDCs to break out of the cycle of debt and poverty is to encourage **fair trade**. This is trade that pays a fair price to the farmers who grow the crops and guarantees a minimum price even when the world market price falls. Of course, this means that consumers in MEDCs – you and I – have to pay more to buy these products in the shops. The alternatives to fair trade are to provide more aid to LEDCs or to do nothing at all.

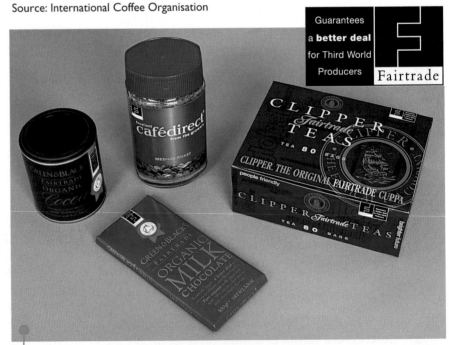

Guarantees a **better deal** for Third World Producers   **Fairtrade**

I The Fairtrade Mark shows that more of the price you pay in shops goes to the people who grow the product.

Activities

1 **a)** Think about the things that the Honduran government needs to spend money on to improve people's quality of life. Make a list of at least ten things.

b) Debt repayments mean that the government has less money to spend on other things.

- What on your list would you cut?
- How would that affect people?

2 Look at sources G and H.
a) Explain what they tell you about the income received by coffee growers.
b) If the price of coffee in the shops goes up, where does most of the extra money go? How do you feel about this?

Homework

3 Carry out some research into fair trade products.
a) At your local supermarket, find out the normal price of products such as coffee, tea and bananas. Does the supermarket also sell fair trade products (see photo I)? If so, how much do they cost?
b) Interview your family or friends to find out whether they know about fair trade products. Would they be prepared to change their shopping habits to buy fair trade products? What reasons do they give?

Assignment

How should we help Honduras develop?

In October 1998 Honduras, along with its Central American neighbours, was devastated by Hurricane Mitch. It was the worst hurricane to hit the region in living memory. About 6,000 people in Honduras died in the floods and mudslides that followed the hurricane and 800,000 people were made homeless. It was estimated that development in the country was set back by about twenty years. The newspaper extracts below describe some of the problems caused by the hurricane.

1 With the help of drawing B on page 38, make a labelled map of Honduras showing how the hurricane affected each part of the country.

2 Write a report for the government of an MEDC that wants to help Honduras to develop after Hurricane Mitch. Divide the report into two sections:
a) short-term aid
b) long-term aid.
Consider the long-term problems of trade and debt in section (b) of your report.

> The swollen Rio Choluteca has turned the centre of Tegucigalpa into a vast lake. The hillsides around the city are strewn with the wreckage of shanty towns.

> In the mountain region, about a quarter of the coffee crop – worth £50 million – has been lost, along with much of the food on which people depend to survive.

J A banana plantation damaged by Hurricane Mitch

> The shrimp industry on the Pacific coast in the south of Honduras has almost been wiped out. The damage could be £45 million.

> Transport through the mountains, which has always been difficult, is now impossible, with bridges destroyed and roads blocked by landslides.

> With hundreds of bodies rotting in the open air, and water supplies disrupted, there are fears of epidemics, including cholera and malaria.

> Many banana plantations around San Pedro Sula and along the Caribbean coast have been flattened by the hurricane.

> When Mitch dumped a record volume of rainfall on the mountains, it led to huge amounts of soil and rock being eroded from hillside farms.

> The richer countries are giving aid to Honduras with one hand and taking it back as debt repayments with the other. The $30 million that the US has given since Hurricane Mitch struck is a lot less than Honduras repaid in debt in 1998.

2.8 Debt in the family . . .

Debt is a problem for many families in Britain – often through no fault of their own.

Most homeowners in Britain have a mortgage – they borrow a proportion of the money needed to buy their home and make monthly payments to the lender. If house prices fall, people may find they owe more money than their home is now worth and they risk losing their home altogether. Or people may be unable to pay business debts, and are said to be bankrupt. When this happens the business is closed down and the remaining debt is cancelled.

A During an **economic boom** people buy homes. Later they may be left with the problem of debt.

In the 1980s Britain had an economic boom. It was easy to borrow money.

Good morning, Mr Burden. Yes, of course we'd be happy to give you a mortgage for a house. Would you like to borrow money for a car as well?

We need more space for the kids.

House prices are going up. It should be a good time to buy.

Everyone's building houses. Loads of work for me. I'll buy a new van and take on some workers.

By the 1990s the economy was in **recession**.

I'm sorry, Mr Burden. I'd like to help you but we've got no more money to lend you.

We've got to pay for the house. Where's the money going to come from?

Don't ask me. The business is struggling.

Sorry, Tel. No one is buying the houses. I can't pay you for the work till we sell them.

But I've got bills to pay and people that need their wages.

People who could not pay their debts lost their homes or their businesses.

Mr Burden, we have given you as much time as we can to repay. I'm afraid the matter is out of our hands.

Say good-bye to the house, kids. We'll be staying with grandma.

This court declares you bankrupt. You cannot run a business for the next five years.

B A tale of two debts

... and debt around the world

Just as individuals and businesses borrow money, most governments borrow money from large international banks to pay for development. This is true for MEDCs as well as for LEDCs. The banks charge interest on these loans, which has to be repaid. However, it is usually the poorer LEDCs – the **heavily indebted poor countries** (HIPCs) – that struggle to repay the debts. They are caught in a trap. The money they owe, in many cases, is more than the money they earn. But a country cannot be declared bankrupt. They are expected to continue to repay their debts.

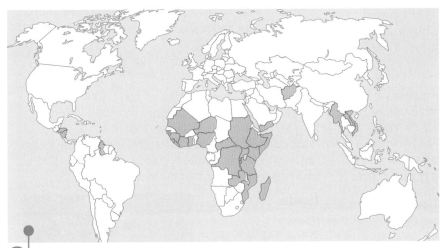

C The world's heavily indebted poor countries

Activities

1 Read cartoon strip B. Describe:
   a) the causes of debt for a family
   b) the consequences of this debt.

2 Look at map C.
   a) Name as many of the world's HIPCs as you can. Check their names in an atlas.
   b) Choose one HIPC and suggest why it is heavily indebted.

3 Read the countdown to debt in source D.
   a) Draw your own cartoon strip to illustrate the processes that led to international debt.
   b) Explain how the causes and consequences of international debt are:
   i) similar to, and
   ii) different from
   the individual debt described in cartoon strip B.

Homework

4 Talk to your family, friends or even a friendly bank manager.
   a) Find out more about how loans and mortgages work. (You don't need to ask any personal details!)
   b) Explain the benefits and/or problems of borrowing money.

In 1973 oil-producing countries around the world increased the price of oil. They made more money and deposited it in large international banks.

Banks had more money to lend. They reduced interest rates and encouraged governments to borrow.

Many LEDCs needed to borrow money to pay for development projects, and to pay the higher oil prices!

Much of the money was wasted. It was spent on large-scale projects that did not help ordinary people, and some went straight to corrupt government leaders.

Unlike oil, the prices of many other primary products was falling. The income of many LEDCs fell. When interest rates rose this made it harder to repay debts.

In 1982 Mexico was the first of many LEDCs to tell the banks that it could not afford to repay its debts. The **International Monetary Fund** and **World Bank** (both United Nations organisations) lent more money but with strict conditions to repay debts. Governments had to prove that they could earn money by increasing their exports and reducing spending.

D Countdown to debt

DIGGING DEEPER

Should debt be cancelled?

Assignment

Should Zambia's debt be cancelled?

You work for the government of Zambia, one of the heavily indebted poor countries. You have been asked to prepare a report to persuade banks and other governments to cancel the country's debts (rather like being declared bankrupt).

1 First, put yourself in the position of banks and other governments. What questions might you have before you decide to cancel debts?

Think of at least five questions. Write them down. You can use these as the headings for the paragraphs in your report.

2 Now, put yourself in the position of the people in Zambia. How could you answer the questions of the banks and governments? Use the information on this page to help you. You can also find more information about Zambia on pages 33–5.

Zambia factfile

Zambia was once one of the richest countries in Africa. When you see images like photo E below, you might imagine that the country has always been poor. But, during the 1960s, Zambia had a thriving copper industry that provided the country with a good income. This enabled the government to spend money on things like health and education so that the country developed.

Then, in the 1970s, the world price of copper fell. Zambia borrowed money to pay for development, expecting the price to rise again. But it never did – in fact, it continued to fall.

Zambia still relies on copper for 85 per cent of its income. It is one of the world's most heavily indebted countries: each person in Zambia owes over $700 in debt – as much as they can earn in two years!

E Rural poverty in Zambia

Education

All schools in Zambia now have to charge school fees, so that only people who are better off can afford to educate their children. The proportion of 6–11 year-olds who go to primary school has fallen, with even fewer attending secondary school.

Health

Following many years of improving health standards in Zambia, the infant mortality rate has begun to rise again. Diseases that had disappeared, such as tuberculosis and yellow fever, are making a comeback. Zambia, like other LEDCs, also has a major problem with AIDS.

Trade

HIPCs are encouraged to grow more export crops in order to earn money to pay off debts. These take up farmland that was previously used to grow subsistence crops for local people. Although earnings from agricultural exports have risen in recent years, the cost of imports has risen faster. Zambia now has to import some food for its own people.

F Pineapples being grown for export

Employment

The cutback in spending means that fewer people are employed in government departments, including health and education. With the price of copper so low, the copper mining companies are employing fewer people. Unemployment in Zambia is over 20 per cent and in the Copper Belt it is over 60 per cent.

The Anfield area of Liverpool. Liverpool Football Club's stadium is surrounded by rows of terraced houses.

Most major football clubs in Britain have their stadium in a city. Often they are in areas of older housing, like the Liverpool stadium. Geographers look at features like this to identify patterns in cities.

- In which part of a city would you expect to find this type of area?
- Who might live here?
- Why do you think a football stadium was built here?
- If people were building a football stadium today, would they choose this location? Why?

GROUNDWORK

3.1

Bright lights for bright sparks!

Have you ever thought about going to college or university? It's never too early to start thinking, even if you haven't decided what GCSEs to do yet!

More young people in Britain are now going on to higher education than ever before. Some stay at home and continue to study in their local area. Many others leave home to go to study in another part of the country. For many 18-year-olds this is the first big decision that they have to take on their own. An important part of the decision is to choose a city (and it usually is a city) where they would like to live. Later they will have to find accommodation somewhere in the city. It's surprising how many adults live in the city they first went to as a student. So it's important to get the decision right!

A Oxford has a traditional city-based university. University buildings are scattered around the city.

LIVERPOOL IS THE student city

Well would YOU disagree with 50,000 people?

Imagine arguing with a crowd larger than the one which gathers at Anfield every fortnight, because that's how many students are around the city every year. And in the age bracket 18 - 24, one in four people in Liverpool are students. Any fears of fitting in and being accepted are immediately dispelled.

CAFE JAZBAR

DUKE ST. 公爵街

WADE SMITH

QUIGGINS CENTRE

THE ALTERNATIVE SHOPPING EXPERIENCE
Designer Fashions
Street Wear
Records Posters
CAFE
ANTIQUES
Bought & Sold

"... this city will cater for your every need and desire"

>>>>>>>>>>>>>>>>>>>>

Liverpool is a compact city, with the centre a tightly-knit jumble of dual-carriageways, pedestrianised streets and short-cut alleys, and with JMU very prominent wherever you look. A quick glance at the map tells you that, with the exception of our IM Marsh campus, all our buildings are located right in the city centre. However, Marsh-ians have regular bus and train services to get them right in the mix of things within ten minutes. JMU students really feel like an integral part of the city, and are welcomed as such by the locals. There are so many students in Liverpool that they represent a large chunk of the local economy, and everybody in the city is well aware of that contribution so students are treated very well.

B Extracts from the prospectus for John Moores University in Liverpool

C | The modern campus at Surrey University. On a campus all the university buildings, including accommodation, are on one large site.

Activities

1 Look at photos A and C.
  a) In which part of the city do you think the two universities are located? Explain how you can tell this from the photos.
  b) List benefits and problems of each type of location.
  c) Suggest why most universities are located in or near cities.

2 Look at source B.
  a) How is the prospectus trying to attract young people to this university?
  b) Write a paragraph to attract students to your nearest town or city.

3 Think about your priorities if you were choosing a city to live in. There are some ideas in the box below. List all your requirements in order of priority.

good shopping   easy access to places in the city
safe streets   cheap accommodation
lively entertainment
good transport links within the UK
multi-racial community   attractive environment
quiet neighbourhood   Premier league football team

4 Work in a group, or with your whole class.
  a) Look at map D. On your own, write one word to describe your image of five cities you have never been to.

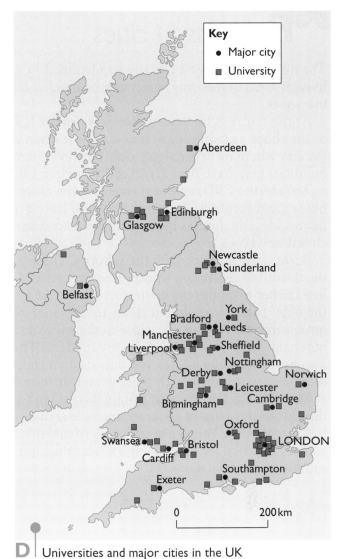

D | Universities and major cities in the UK

  b) How many of these cities have people in your group visited? Each person should describe the cities they know to the rest of the group.
     Compare what other people say to the images you have.
  c) Have any of your images changed?
     Which city would you most like to go to?

Homework

5 Choose one city you would like to know more about.

Carry out some research with the help of your library or the Internet. What would you like to know before you chose a city to live in?

FRAMEWORK

3.2

Patterns in cities

The different parts of a city can be identified by the main land uses in each area. In this way, a city can be divided into separate **land-use zones**.

At the centre is the **central business district (CBD)**, where most of the shops and offices are found. This is often the oldest part of the city where its original site was. However, many of the old buildings may have been replaced by modern office blocks.

Around the CBD, and next oldest, is the **inner city** – an area of houses and factories. This area may also have been modernised in many cities, the houses improved or replaced and the factories closed down.

Beyond the inner city are the **suburbs**. These grew throughout the twentieth century as transport improved and people began to live further from the city centre. As cities tend to grow outwards, the older suburbs are found closer to the inner city. These are the inner suburbs. Further out, close to the edge of the city, are the outer suburbs, where the houses are modern. The outer suburbs also have industrial estates and out-of-town shopping centres, built to replace or compete with those nearer the city centre.

Many towns and cities in Britain have a land-use pattern like this. From this pattern geographers have created an **urban model** (see diagram B). This is a simple way to understand cities. Of course, all cities are more complex than this, but it is often useful to simplify real life.

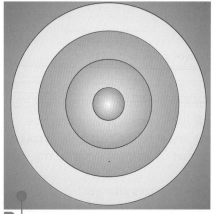

B An urban model to show the land-use pattern in a city

A The growth of Bristol in maps

Key

🐾 Original site of town

1850

1900

1950

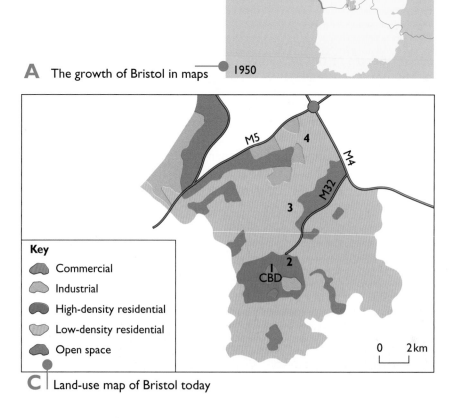

Key

🔴 Commercial

🔵 Industrial

🔴 High-density residential

🔵 Low-density residential

🔵 Open space

C Land-use map of Bristol today

D

E

F

G

Activities

1 Look at diagram B.

  a) On a large copy of the model, label the four parts of the city:
CBD, inner city, inner suburbs and outer suburbs.

  b) Beside the labels, describe the main features in each area.

    For example: The CBD has the oldest buildings, modern office blocks and shops.

2 Look at the maps in source A and map C.

  a) Describe the way that Bristol has grown. Mention its size, the directions in which it has grown and the timescale.

  b) Describe the land-use pattern on map C.

  c) Compare the maps with the model in B. Has Bristol grown as the model shows?

    Suggest why it has grown in the way it has.

3 Look at photos D to G. They show buildings in different parts of Bristol.

  a) Match each photo with one of the four parts of the city and with the locations numbered on map C.

  b) Estimate the date of the oldest buildings in each photo. Choose from: 1820, 1890, 1930, 1990.

  c) Draw labelled sketches of two of the photos to compare the buildings in two areas.

    Choose words from the box below for your labels. Add more labels of your own.

> terraced house　detached house　shops
> semi-detached house　double-glazed windows
> garage　on-road parking　small garden
> large garden　no garden　old windows

Homework

4 Think about your nearest town or city. Name at least one area that matches each of the four zones in the city: the CBD, inner city, inner suburbs and outer suburbs.

  Mark the location of each area on a simple sketch map of the town or city. You could cut out adverts for houses in different areas from local papers and stick them around your map.

  How well does your town or city match the model?

FRAMEWORK

3.3 Changing land-use patterns

Land-use patterns in many cities are changing. This can happen as the functions of the city change. (You may have studied the functions of settlements in *Earthworks 1*.)

In some cities, old factories and docks in the inner city closed down, leaving the land **derelict**. In recent years, some of these areas have been **redeveloped** by building new housing and attracting new industries.

Meanwhile, new outer suburbs are growing due to increases in car ownership and improvements in road transport. People and businesses moved beyond the older suburbs to new residential areas and industrial or commercial sites beyond the edge of the city. The loss of countryside to urban land use is called **suburbanisation**.

A | Typical land use in a city in the 1970s

B | The docks in London were still busy in 1968.

I worked in the docks until they closed in 1980. Until then I'd spent my whole life living and working in the area. Soon after, we got the chance to buy the house that we'd been renting for twenty years. We used all the money they gave me when I lost my job.

Then when they started to redevelop the docks, everything began to change. Most of our friends left the area and new people started moving in with their money. We were able to sell our house and move out to be nearer the country. Now I don't think I'd want to move back. I never thought I'd be saying that twenty years ago!

C | The story of a family in the inner city

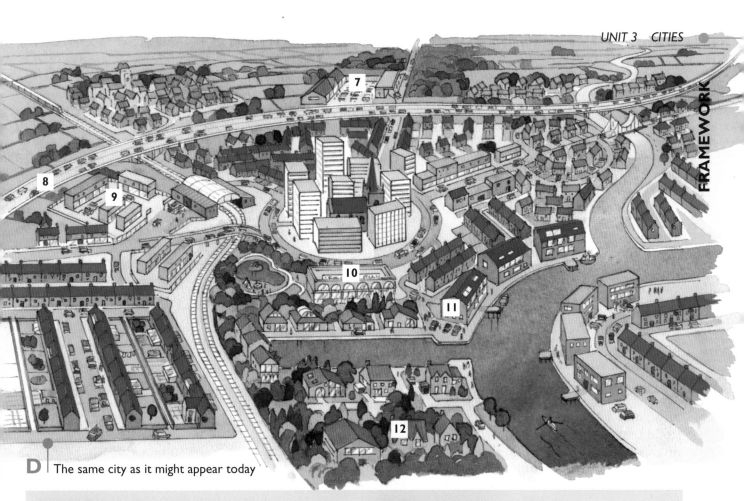

D The same city as it might appear today

Activities

1 Look at drawings A and D.
   a) Identify each of the following features on one
   of the two drawings. Match them to a number
   on the drawings.

   > terraced housing   industrial estate   village
   > luxury housing   converted warehouse flats   factory
   > motorway   out-of-town shopping centre   CBD   dock
   > suburbs   office development

   b) Compare the two drawings. Identify at least
   ten changes that have taken place.
   c) Write two paragraphs describing the changes
   that have happened as a result of:
   i) urban redevelopment
   ii) suburbanisation.

2 Read the experiences of the family in C. Then
   look at photos B and E.
   a) Suggest changes that might have happened in
   the area shown in photo B since the photo
   was taken.
   b) Suggest what changes had happened in the
   area shown in E before the photo was taken.
   c) Explain what impact these changes had on the
   life of the family in C.

E Old houses in the inner city have been improved

3 What impact might the changing land-use patterns
   have had on the following people since the 1970s?
   Write a short biography for each person.
   Describe their life before and how it has changed.
   a) a farmer near the edge of the city
   b) a shop-owner in the CBD
   c) a school-leaver living in the inner city
   d) a university graduate moving to the city in the
   1980s. (Begin this biography with the move to
   the city.)

51

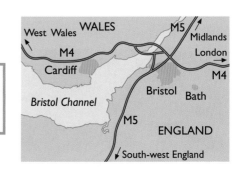

West Wales WALES M5 Midlands
M4 London
Cardiff M4
Bristol Bath
Bristol Channel
M5 ENGLAND
South-west England

BUILDING BLOCKS

In this Building Block you will use maps, photos, data and personal opinions to compare the quality of life in three areas of Bristol.

3.4

Does it matter where you live in the city?

Bristol, in the south-west of England, is a large city with a population of 370,000. It grew as a port on the River Avon. The intersection of the M4 and M5 motorways is close to Bristol.

Tanisha, Nick and Jack are pupils at the Mary Redcliffe and Temple School near the centre of Bristol. They have been asked to carry out a geographical investigation to compare quality of life in different parts of the city.

A Tanisha lives in Montpelier.

B Nick lives in Horfield.

C Jack lives in Bradley Stoke.

Activities

1 Look at photos A–C and map extract D.
   a) Locate the Mary Redcliffe and Temple School at grid reference 596 720. (It is not labelled on the map.)
   b) The three pupils live at the following grid references:
      589 763   623 808   597 744
      Match each grid reference with the correct pupil.
   c) Work out the best route for each pupil to get to school.
      Measure how far they have to travel. Describe the route they would take.
   d) Suggest reasons why the pupils go to this school when the map shows that there are other schools closer to where they live.

2 a) For each pupil, find out from the map how good their access to services is. Measure the distance from their home to the nearest

   • school   • hospital   • railway station.

Pupil	Nearest school		Nearest hospital		Nearest railway station	
	Grid reference	Distance	Grid reference	Distance	Grid reference	Distance

   b) Complete a table like the one above. Which pupil appears to have the best access to services?

3 Draw a simple sketch map of the area of Bristol shown on map D. Use a large outline grid, like the one on the right, to help you. On your map, show:
   a) motorways and major roads
   b) the main built-up area
   c) railways and stations
   d) the pupils' homes and their school.

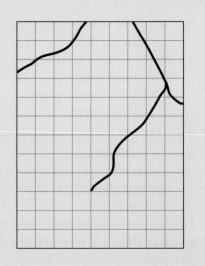

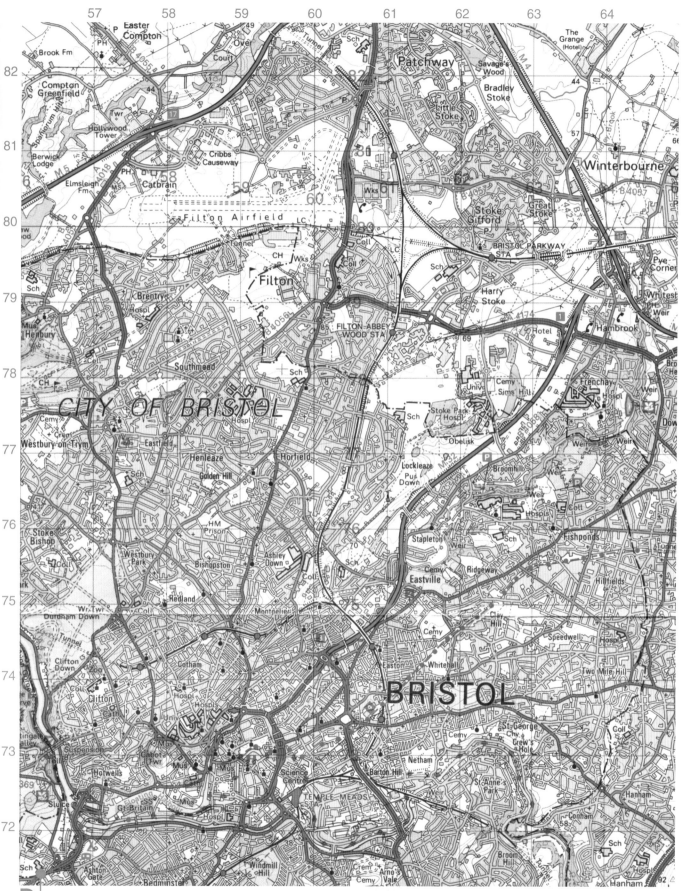

D Bristol city centre and the north-east of the city. Reproduced from the 1997 1:50,000 Ordnance Survey map by permission of the Controller of HMSO © Crown Copyright.

How does the quality of life differ?

Some people say they wouldn't like to live in Montpelier; it has the reputation of being a rough part of Bristol. I like it, though. It's got a good community feeling and there are places for young people to go.
Every July we have a festival. They block off the roads and there is a parade. That's the best thing that happens here. The worst things are the litter and the crime. It's easy to get to school from here, and to the city centre. You can walk if you want, but I'd rather go on a bus!

E Montpelier, the area where Tanisha lives. It is in the Ashley ward of the city.

Horfield seems a pretty ordinary place to me. Just rows of semi-detached houses and not much to do. There seem to be lots of old people here and families with young kids, but not so many teenagers.
Most of the shops we need are just round the corner on the Gloucester Road. There's also a new Tesco supermarket that has opened quite near by. But if you want to do anything exciting – like ice-skating, bowling, even the cinema – you have to go to the city centre.

F Horfield, the ward where Nick lives

Living in Bradley Stoke is a bit like living on a building site. When it's finished there will be about 10,000 homes here. That'll be a lot of people! They say it's the largest new development in Europe.
They've got all sorts of plans for the area, but I'll probably have left by the time they happen. At the moment there isn't even a secondary school, so I go all the way to Mary Redcliffe and Temple. Hardly any of my school friends live round here, so it's hard to get to know anyone. New people are always moving in.

G Bradley Stoke South, the area where Jack lives

Activity

For this activity, use all the information in this Building Block, including sources H and I on the page opposite and the photos on page 49.

a) If you lived in Bristol, decide in which of the three areas you would be most likely to do each of the things in the box on the right:

b) In each case, think of reasons for your answer.

c) If you lived in Bristol, in which of the three areas would you choose to live? Why?

let children play outside on the street
park your car in a garage
buy food in a Caribbean shop
need double-glazing to reduce traffic noise
live in the same street all your life
get behind with the rent
pay the largest heating bills
go for a bike ride in the countryside
replace the old roof on your house
spend the weekend gardening
take a taxi back from the shops
hear football crowds

		Ashley	Horfield	Bradley Stoke South
Population change 1981–91		−5.17	−4.51	No population in 1981
Population:	Under 15	21	18	16
	Over 65	10.5	14	3
	Ethnic minorities	29	5	No data
	Single-parent households	38	12	1.6
Employment:	In work	49.8	53.4	75.0
	Unemployed	14.0	4.2	3.6
	Retired	13.1	22.2	4.6
	Student	5.6	3.9	1.5
Housing tenure:	Owner-occupied	49.8	68.2	95.5
	Public rented	34.4	26.4	0.3
	Private rented	15.8	5.4	3.9
Amenities:	Central heating	71.6	79.9	100.0
	One or more car	52.2	69.6	96.9

The pupils were able to make their own observations of the areas where they lived. They took photos, interviewed people and recorded information about things like land use and services in their own area. These are **primary sources**.

They were also able to obtain maps and data about different parts of Bristol from the local library and planning department. This provided information that it would be difficult for them to find for themselves, for example, housing **tenure** (whether people own or rent their homes). These are **secondary sources**.

H   Data comparing three wards or areas in Bristol. This is a secondary source. All figures given are percentages.
Source: Bristol City Council, *Ward Report*, 1991

Assignment

How does quality of life change as you move out from the city centre?
Do *either* this assignment, *or* the local investigation below.

You are going to compare the quality of life in the three areas of Bristol to test the hypothesis: *quality of life improves as you move out from the city centre*. Use all the information in this Building Block and on pages 48–9 to help you.

- Think about how to organise your comparison. You could divide it into sections under different headings. For example: *housing, population, environmental quality*, etc.
- Then, think about how to present your findings. You could draw a large table, make a display or do a written comparison divided into sections.
- Write up your conclusions. Is the hypothesis correct? If not, rewrite it to be more accurate.

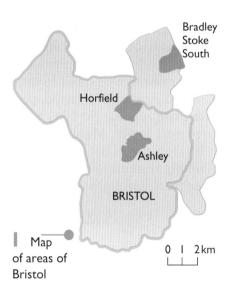

I   Map of areas of Bristol

0   1   2km

Local investigation

How does quality of life change as you move out from the city centre?
Do *either* this investigation, *or* the assignment above.

You are going to carry out a local investigation into the quality of life in your nearest town or city.

- Think of a question to investigate, or a hypothesis to test. It does not need to be the same one as in Bristol.

- Plan how you will carry out the investigation. What primary and secondary sources will you use? You could include interviews and take your own photos as primary sources.
- Present the results of your investigation. You could make a display in your classroom.
- Write up your conclusions.

In this Building Block you will learn from mistakes made by planners in London's Docklands and then make your own plans.

3.5 How should Docklands be redeveloped?

Do planners ever learn from their mistakes? People living in the London Docklands area believe many mistakes have been made since redevelopment began in 1981. Now the focus of redevelopment has moved downstream to the Royal Docks in Newham and people there hope that history won't be repeated.

In 1981 London's Docklands was an urban area in serious decline. The docks, which had been part of a thriving port employing thousands of local people, stood empty. Many of the industries associated with the docks, like ship repairers and flour mills, closed down leaving the area with the highest unemployment in London.

Then the government stepped in, setting up the London Docklands Development Corporation (LDDC), the first **Urban Development Corporation**.

For eighteen years the LDDC brought land and buildings back into use, often with the help of private development companies. New roads and a light railway were built to improve transport. New industry was attracted, particularly into the **enterprise zone** on the Isle of Dogs, as rent and rates were lower. Many new homes were built.

In 1998 the LDDC was wound up and planning responsibility was handed back to the three local boroughs in the Docklands area.

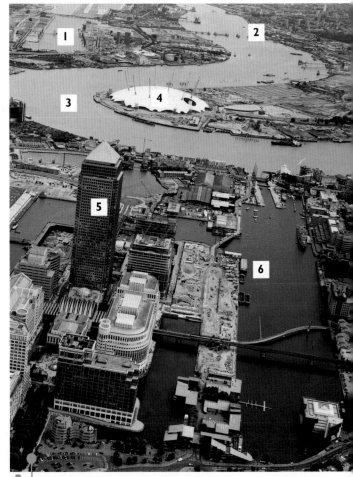

A London's Docklands and the River Thames

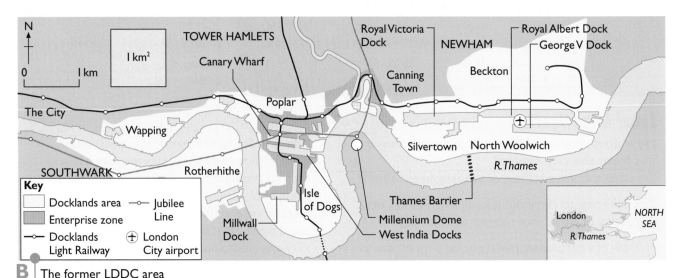

B The former LDDC area

Key
- ☐ Docklands area
- ▨ Enterprise zone
- —o— Docklands Light Railway
- —o— Jubilee Line
- ⊕ London City airport

The Docklands Light Railway provides easy transport to the Isle of Dogs.

Canary Wharf, location of London's tallest building. Many banks, insurance companies and newspapers have offices here.

The docks are at the centre of the enterprise zone that attracted new business to the area.

New housing occupies most of the land close to the river. There is a mixture of old and new housing in the area.

Local services are limited. The Isle of Dogs has one major supermarket to serve the 20,000 people who live there.

A few areas of derelict land remain where factories once stood. These will be used for more housing.

C The Isle of Dogs in 1999 – redevelopment is almost complete.

Activities

1 Compare photo A with map B.
a) Match the following features to the numbers on the photo:

> River Thames   West India Docks
> Royal Victoria Dock   Canary Wharf
> Thames Barrier   Millennium Dome

b) In which direction was the camera pointing when this photo was taken? How can you tell?
c) Photos A and C were both taken from the air. Explain the difference between them.

2 Look at map B.
a) i) Use the scale to measure the length of London's Docklands area from east to west.
   ii) Estimate the total area of London's Docklands.

3 Look carefully at photo C.
a) Identify each of the main land-use areas. How can you tell the difference between housing and industrial/commercial areas on the photo?

b) Draw an outline sketch map of the photo to show the main land-use areas.
   Show areas of housing, industry/commerce, open space and water and transport. (Don't try to show individual buildings.)
   Colour your map and give it a key.
c) Estimate the percentage of the total area occupied by each land use on the Isle of Dogs.

4 Look at pie chart D.
a) Estimate the percentage occupied by each land use in 1981.
b) Draw a table to compare land use on the Isle of Dogs in 1981 and 1999.
c) Describe how land use in the area changed.

Housing

Water and transport

Open space/ derelict

Industry

D   Land use on the Isle of Dogs in 1981

Who will redevelopment be for?

I've lived in this area all my life. Once upon a time it was a thriving community. Men used to work in the docks and there were more local factories. When the docks closed, it wasn't just jobs that went – the area lost its sense of pride. Lots of people left the area, shops were boarded up, we began to see more vandalism. We've even had a number of suicides – mainly youngsters. It's tragic.

The trouble with these new plans for the Royal Docks is that they don't do anything for local people. We've seen the Isle of Dogs turn into a rich man's playground. What we need is jobs for local people, better transport and more local services. We opened this laundrette ourselves because the nearest one is twenty minutes away on the bus. But we still have no library, no bank and few shops. This area has been forgotten.

E Connie Hunt, a resident of North Woolwich

We live in a one-bedroom apartment overlooking the old docks. We moved here because it seemed the nicest place to live in east London. Sitting on the balcony, it's so peaceful you'd never know you were in the city. But we're also close to our work. Because we are both working as teachers we can afford the rent, which is over £600 a month. But prices are going up and we are worried that our landlord may decide to sell. The flat might cost about £120,000 to buy and that would be too much for us.

F Geoff and Mohni recently moved into their new Docklands apartment.

Activities

1 Read what Connie Hunt says in source E. How might the closure of the docks have led to:
   a) shops closing
   b) an increase in vandalism
   c) suicides?

2 Read what Geoff and Mohni say in source F.
   a) Imagine you are an estate agent. Design an advert to sell an apartment like this.
      Think about all the things you would mention. For example: household amenities, location and the local environment.
   b) Who would want to buy an apartment like this? Who could afford it?

3 People who move to Docklands may have different needs from people who have always lived there.
   a) Think about what each group might need. Which ideas in the box would benefit each group? Would some ideas benefit everybody?

schools supermarkets parks airport hospital luxury apartments factories and workshops public transport yachting marina cheap housing sports centre local services, e.g. library offices and information services good roads specialist shops university

   b) Draw a Venn diagram (as below) to show:
      i) things that those who have always lived in the area need
      ii) things that newcomers need
      iii) things that both groups need (in the centre).
      You could include more ideas of your own.

The plans for the Royal Docks area in Newham make it one of the largest urban redevelopment projects in Europe. It consists of 120 hectares of mainly derelict land, surrounding 80 hectares of water. The area is already served by all the major forms of transport: road, rail, air and water.

Redevelopment in the Royal Docks is the final phase in the redevelopment of London Docklands. It offers an opportunity to learn from mistakes that were made in the redevelopment of the neighbouring Isle of Dogs. These mistakes included:

- lack of affordable housing for people already living in the area
- lack of jobs to replace those that were lost when the docks and old industries closed down
- inadequate transport to meet the needs of people living in the area and people travelling to the area for work.

The Royal Docks area includes a new campus for the University of East London, London City Airport and a new exhibition centre for London. Critics point out that these prestige projects are not local priorities, and they need to be balanced by development that meets local needs.

G London City Airport is mainly used by business travellers to Europe.

H An old shopping parade in North Woolwich. The nearest supermarket is 4 kilometres away.

Assignment

How should West Silvertown Urban Village be redeveloped?

Work in a small group.
You have been asked to make detailed plans for West Silvertown Urban Village, part of the Royal Docks area.

1 Study the information on these two pages and use the Venn diagram you completed in activity 3b. Think about how you could meet the needs of everyone who lives in or uses the area.

2 Write a report to show how you would meet people's needs in the area.
Include a large-scale plan for West Silvertown Urban Village in your report. Your teacher will give you a large outline map of the area. Mark your plans for each land use – housing, industry, transport, open space, etc. – on the map.

I Major redevelopments in the Royal Docks

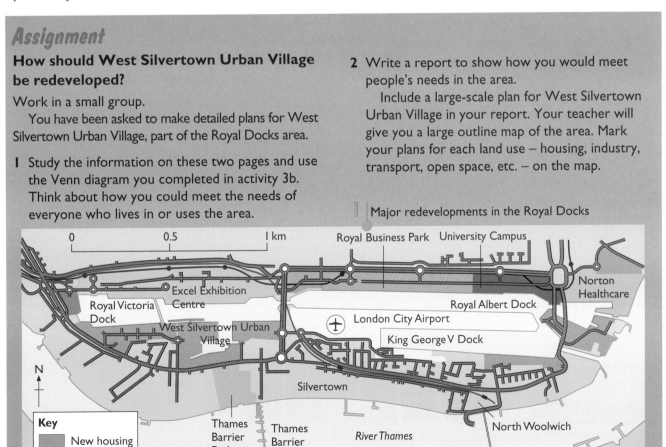

In this Building Block you will investigate changing land-use patterns in Chicago and design a new urban model.
This will also help you with the USA investigation on page 107.

3.6 How has the American city changed?

A The centre of Chicago in the 1920s

The first urban land-use model was based on the American city of Chicago in the 1920s. It was Burgess' **concentric ring model**, named after the person who proposed it. It was based on the idea that all cities grow outwards from their centre. As they grow, a number of zones emerge, each with their own characteristic land use and population. Burgess' model could be applied to other cities in the USA and elsewhere.

Key

Central Business District – contains the main shops and offices and is the focus for major transport routes.

Transition zone – contains the oldest housing and light industry. Most residents here are usually poor people and new immigrants.

Low-class residential zone – poor-quality housing. Working-class people live close to the factories where they work.

Medium-class residential zone – higher-quality housing where middle-class people live.

High-class residential zone – high-quality housing where the wealthiest people live. They can afford to travel further to work.

B Burgess' concentric ring model

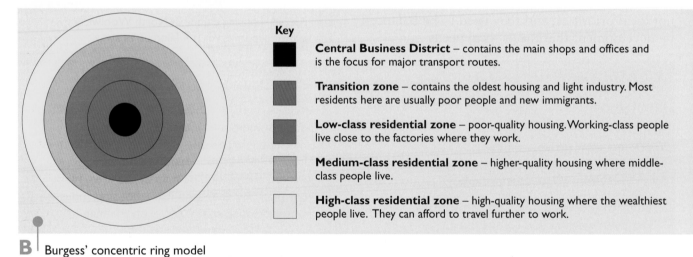

C An urban cross-section showing how land values and population change with distance from the city centre

In practice, it was found that land-use patterns did not fit the Burgess model in all cities. In the 1930s Hoyt devised an alternative urban land-use model, based on the study of many cities in the USA. This was the **sector model**.

Hoyt found that some land uses radiate out from the city centre in the shape of a sector, or wedge. Often these were focused on major transport routes that attract commerce or industry.

D Commercial growth along a modern American highway

E Hoyt's sector model

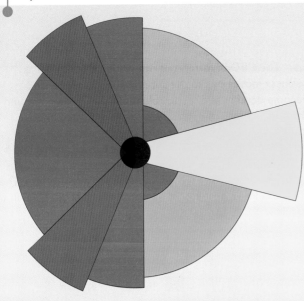

To keep their models simple, Burgess and Hoyt assumed that:

- the city was built on a flat surface (they ignored physical features like hills or rivers)
- each zone had clear boundaries
- there was only one main land use in each zone
- there were no planning laws to restrict where people were allowed to build
- people could not live too far from the city centre because transport was slow

Activities

1 Compare photos A and D.
   a) Describe the ways in which American cities have changed since the 1920s.
   b) Suggest how these changes could affect the land-use pattern in a city.

2 Look at land-use models B and E.
   a) Describe two similarities and two differences between the two models.
   b) Compare both models to a British city that you have studied.
   Which model *best* fits the land-use pattern in that city? Explain your answer.

3 a) Look at diagram C. Describe how:
   i) land values   ii) population
   change as you move out from the city centre.
   b) Now compare land values with the height of buildings in the city. Explain the link.
   c) Use box B and diagram C to compare population with the types of building in the city. Explain the link that you find.

4 Read the list of assumptions in box E.
   a) Suggest five ways in which real cities today are different from this.
   b) If real cities are different to the models does this mean that the models are not useful? Explain your answer.

Is there a new urban model?

F   Due to the high level of car ownership in the USA, American cities are often very large. Around the edge of the city lies kilometre upon kilometre of suburban development, or **urban sprawl**. The typical American suburb consists of low-density housing – large detached homes each in its own plot of land. This means that people have to travel long distances to reach the city centre or their nearest shopping centre. Often there is no public transport service, so people have to depend on their cars.

G   The CBD in many American cities is in decline as business moves out to the suburbs. Buildings and land become derelict and the problem of crime grows. Around the CBD some old inner-city areas have turned into **ghettos** – areas of high-density housing which are often run-down and overcrowded. These are usually inhabited by black people or other ethnic minority groups. Many came here when they first arrived in the USA as immigrants. They are often in low-paid jobs, so cannot afford the houses in the suburbs.

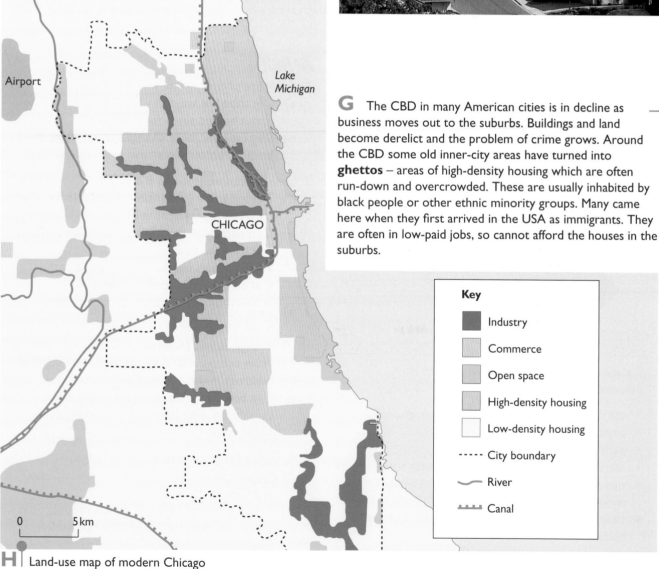

Key

- ■ Industry
- ▨ Commerce
- ▨ Open space
- ▨ High-density housing
- □ Low-density housing
- ----- City boundary
- — River
- ▪▪▪▪ Canal

H   Land-use map of modern Chicago

Activities

1 Look at photos F, G and I.
   a) Describe three changes that have happened in American cities, like Chicago, in recent years.
   b) From your knowledge, are similar changes happening in cities in Britain? Give evidence to support your answer.
   c) In each case, do you think these changes are positive or negative? Give reasons for your answers.

2 From map H, describe the land-use pattern in modern Chicago. Think about answering the following questions in your description:

   • Where is the CBD? Are there other commercial areas? Where are they?
   • Where is industry found? Is there a pattern?
   • What residential patterns are there? Where are the high-density residential areas? Where are the low-density areas?

Assignment

Design your own urban model

You are going to draw an urban model based on the information about Chicago on these two pages and on other cities you know. Think about the problems with the models of Burgess and Hoyt. Your answers to activity 4 on page 61 may help you.

• Would your model have concentric rings or sectors?
• What land uses would you find in each zone?
• What is the new pattern?

When you have drawn your model, present it to a group in your class. Describe and explain the main features of the model.
   Consider the models of other members of your group. As a group, can you agree on one urban model that best fits all the cities you know? You may need to combine elements from more than one model.

I Businesses that move from the CBD or inner city often relocate to out-of-town sites. New industrial parks, office parks and shopping malls have grown up around the main highway intersections surrounding the city. These offer modern premises, often at much lower rents than old, cramped sites near the city centre. This is sometimes called the **doughnut effect** – business hops over the suburbs from the CBD to the edge of the city, leaving a 'hole' in the middle.

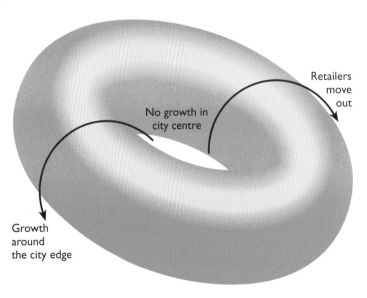

Retailers move out

No growth in city centre

Growth around the city edge

DIGGING DEEPER

3.7
Should we concrete over the countryside?

There is a growing shortage of housing in Britain. The number of households is growing much more quickly than the total population. The main reason is that more people are living on their own. The number of single-person households increased from 18 per cent in 1971 to 29 per cent in 1996. You can see some of the reasons for this in diagram B.

In response to this, the government has said that 4.5 million new homes need to be built by the year 2020. Environmentalists and people living in rural areas fear that this will mean large areas of countryside will disappear under concrete and bricks. Much of this growth is intended for the areas that are already the most crowded.

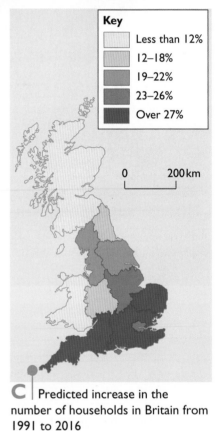

A Many people in Britain live in single-person households.

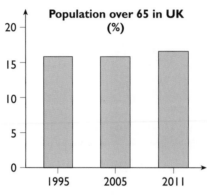

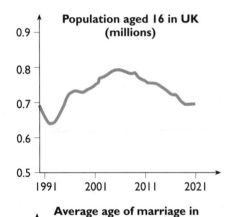

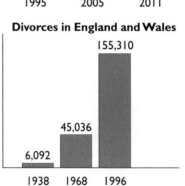

B Population trends in the UK

Key
- Less than 12%
- 12–18%
- 19–22%
- 23–26%
- Over 27%

0   200 km

C Predicted increase in the number of households in Britain from 1991 to 2016

Activities

1 Look at photo A.
   a) Why do you think this student is living alone?
   b) Think of other groups of people that live in single-person households.

2 Study the data in the four graphs in B.
   a) Write four sentences, one about each graph, to describe the trends shown.

   b) Explain how each of these trends could lead to an increase in single-person households.

3 a) Describe the pattern on map C.
   b) Compare this pattern with a map of population density in Britain in your atlas. Which parts of the country are likely to become most crowded? Explain why.

D New development on a greenfield site

For more than 50 years, much of the countryside around British cities has been part of the **green belt**. This is land that is protected by law, where there are restrictions on building. The green belt was first designated to stop urban sprawl and to prevent neighbouring towns and cities from merging into each other.

But this policy is under threat. The pressure to build more homes is so great that green belt land will be lost as houses are built on **greenfield sites**. The alternative is to make better use of derelict land and empty buildings in the cities. These are often called **brownfield sites**.

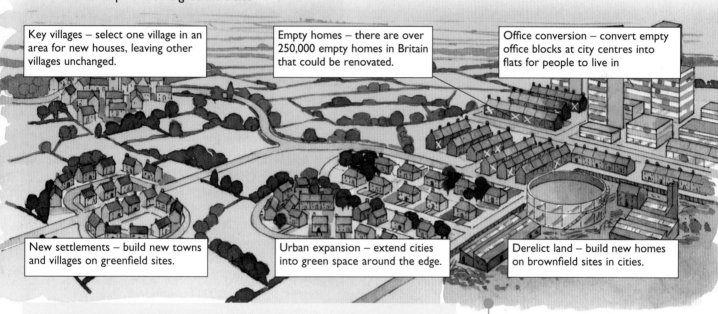

Key villages – select one village in an area for new houses, leaving other villages unchanged.

Empty homes – there are over 250,000 empty homes in Britain that could be renovated.

Office conversion – convert empty office blocks at city centres into flats for people to live in

New settlements – build new towns and villages on greenfield sites.

Urban expansion – extend cities into green space around the edge.

Derelict land – build new homes on brownfield sites in cities.

E Ways to create new homes

4 Look at photos D and F.
  a) Compare the suitability of the two sites for building new homes. Think about space, building costs, service provision (water, electricity, etc.), transport.
  b) Suggest what each of the following people might think about development on each of the two sites:

   • a builder   • an environmentalist   • a house buyer.

5 Look at drawing E. Suggest at least one advantage and one disadvantage of each of the ways to create new homes.
   Complete a table to show the pros and cons of each approach.

Homework

6 Look around your local area. How could more homes be created?
   Would you have to build new homes, or could you use existing buildings?
   Could you develop brownfield sites, or would you have to build on greenfield sites?
   How might other local people feel about these suggestions?

F New housing on a brownfield site

DIGGING DEEPER

Good-bye to the green belt?

Assignment

Where shall we build new houses?

Work in a small group. You are members of the planning authority in Cambridgeshire. You have been asked by the government to decide where in the county to build 70,000 new homes by the year 2020.

You have four main options to consider.

A) Refuse to co-operate with the government, but then they will probably take the decision for you.

B) Spread the new development around the county in existing towns and villages.

C) Build new settlements on greenfield sites, such as the new town already proposed for Cambourne.

D) Build new homes on brownfield sites, such as the development already proposed for Oakington.

Study all the information on this page and on pages 64–5. Decide which of these options you will choose. Think about the effect your decisions will have on people already living in Cambridgeshire. Write a letter to the government to explain your decision.

CAMBRIDGE BLUES OVER NEW DEVELOPMENT PLANS

Proposals for a privately-funded new town of 50,000 outside Cambridge could lead to similar developments in the overcrowded South-east, the government believes.

With a higher-than-expected population growth early in the next century, the Deputy Prime Minister, John Prescott, will shortly be forced to revise estimates of housing demand. New figures project the population in Britain at 61.9 million by 2016 – almost a million higher than previous estimates. With the rising demand for one-person properties, government sources say that 5 million new homes could be needed.

Such a level of building will meet resistance. It would be 'a disaster' for the countryside said Tony Burton of the Council for the Protection of Rural England. With county councils from West Sussex to Cambridgeshire resisting expansion, ministers say that new settlements could be preferable to piecemeal growth.

A senior minister welcomed the Cambridge proposal, and said, 'New towns could well be the solution in particular regions, like the South-east, where there is a big demand for houses caused by the expansion of cities like Cambridge.'

If approved, Cambridge New Town, on the site of an old airfield just outside the city's cherished green belt at Oakington, will be the first one of its kind for 40 years. Significantly, the site fulfils some of the conditions laid down by the government for new house building because it is classed as 'brownfield'. Mr Prescott has set a target to build 60 per cent of new homes on brownfield sites.

H Extract adapted from the *Guardian*, 17 October 1998

> This is a real village, and I couldn't imagine a whole new set of houses here. We've had our fair share and you can't keep endlessly adding to villages like this. Something has to snap.

G Jean Coston, a Cambridgeshire councillor in Waterbeach

Four possible sites for development in Cambridgeshire

1 Oakington. Redundant Ministry of Defence barracks. Proposal for a new town with 50,000 population.

2 Waterbeach. Redundant barracks. Proposed new settlement with 20,000 population.

3 Wyton. Former airfield. Proposal for a new settlement with 10,000 population.

4 Cambourne. Greenfield site. Proposal for a new settlement with 10,000 population to include a business park and shopping centre.

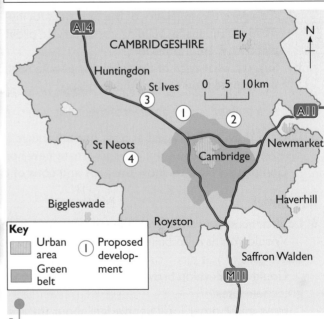

I Four possible sites for development in Cambridgeshire

UNIT 4 ENERGY RESOURCES –
What has global warming got to do with you?

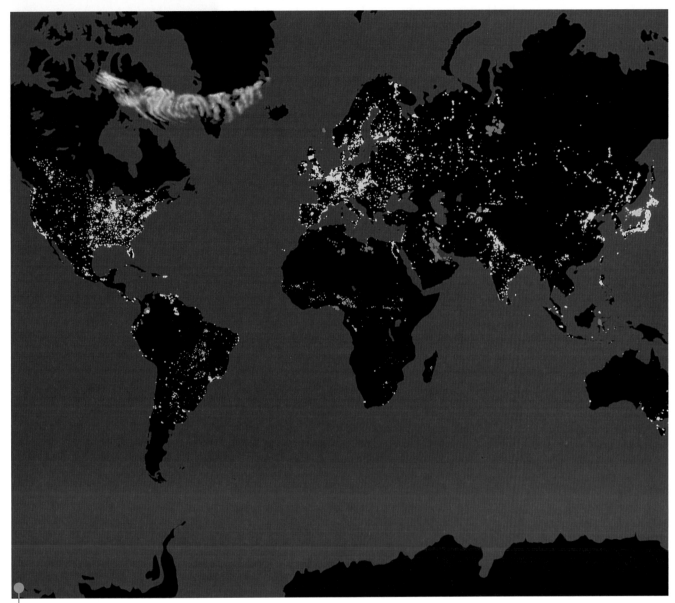

A satellite image of the world. The areas of yellow light show human settlement and indicate how much **energy** is being used. Purple light comes from areas of forest fires, green light from night-time Japanese fishing fleets and red light from natural gas flares. The band of light at the top of the map is the Northern Lights, a natural phenomenon that is nothing to do with human activity.

- Which parts of the world are using most energy? How many cities can you identify?
- How does the image compare to a world map of population distribution?
- Do any parts of the world appear to be using less energy than you might expect? Which ones? Can you suggest why?

GROUNDWORK

Last one out, please switch off the lights!

Did you know that schools in Britain spend three times as much money on energy as on books? A typical secondary school spends about £40,000 a year on its fuel bills, so it makes good sense to save energy. Think how many books a school could buy if it used just ten per cent less energy!

But there are other reasons for wanting to conserve, or save, energy. Most of our energy comes from burning **fossil fuels** – mainly oil, gas and coal. Your school probably burns one of these fuels in its boiler to provide heating and hot water. The rest of the energy the school uses comes from electricity, which is often produced by burning fossil fuels. Eventually the world will run out of fossil fuels, so we need to use them carefully for the sake of future generations. What's more, people all over the world burning fuel is having a major impact on the global environment.

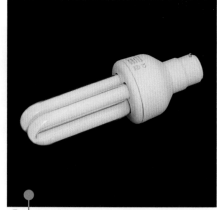

A Fluorescent lamps can save energy and reduce fuel bills.

Glass-fibre insulation between the ceiling and outer roof

Roof 22%

Double glazing on windows

HOW TO SAVE ENERGY

Ventilation 35%

It's too hot to work today Miss

Windows 26%

Walls 9%

Floors 8%

Draught excluder around windows and doors

Thermostatic controls on radiators prevent the classroom getting too hot (or too cold!)

Wall cavities filled with foam

B Heat loss from a classroom and energy **conservation** methods to reduce this loss. The arrows show the percentage of total heat loss.

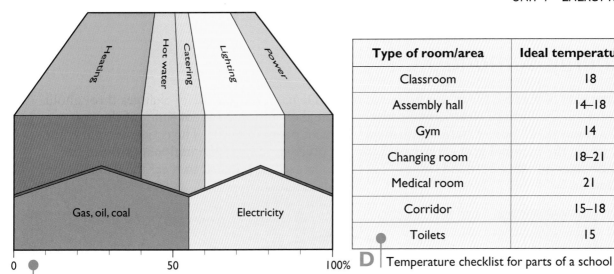

Type of room/area	Ideal temperature (°C)
Classroom	18
Assembly hall	14–18
Gym	14
Changing room	18–21
Medical room	21
Corridor	15–18
Toilets	15

D | Temperature checklist for parts of a school

C | Energy used in a school

Activities

1 Think about your own school.
  a) List all the ways in which energy is used there.
  b) Have you noticed any ways in which the school tries to save energy?

2 Look at drawing B.
  a) Identify five ways in which energy is being wasted.
  b) Draw a graph or diagram to show how heat is lost from this classroom.
  c) Suggest what actions to save energy could be taken by:
    i) pupils and teachers
    ii) the site supervisor
    iii) the school governors (who decide how money is spent).

3 Look at diagram C.
  a) Estimate the percentage of energy in a school that is:
    i) used for each purpose
    ii) from each source.
  b) Complete a table to show the information.
  c) Suggest ways for a school to make savings on:
    i) its fuel bill
    ii) its electricity bill.

4 Carry out a temperature check around your school.
  a) Walk around the school to record the temperature in each area. This is best done with an electronic sensor.
  b) Compare the temperatures you recorded with those in table D. Colour a school plan to show temperatures in each area. Indicate areas that are warmer or colder than they should be.

  c) Write a short report to suggest how energy, and therefore money, could be saved at your school. Give a copy to your headteacher.

5 Saving energy is not just about money. Look at photo E. Here is a mystery for you! How could energy conservation help to save polar bears? Think about this as you study the rest of the unit. We will come back to this later on.

E |

Homework

6 Do some research into energy use in your home.
  a) Find out how much your family spends on energy each month or quarter (three months). How does this vary from one quarter to another?
  b) Suggest ways that your family could conserve energy to reduce energy bills.

4.2

Energy demand ...

Much of the energy that we use in our homes and schools comes in the form of electricity, produced in **power stations**. Each power station transmits energy to us via the **national grid** – a network of transmission lines and underground cables crossing Britain.

Demand for electricity changes throughout the day, and at different times of the year, to meet people's needs. The energy output from power stations to the national grid can be increased or reduced to meet the demand for electricity.

A Energy demand on a typical winter weekday in Britain

B Mr Jones puts the kettle on.

• Carol catches the train home during the rush hour.
• Bethan gets up early to have a shower.
• Bryn goes to the school cafeteria for a hot lunch.
• David turns on the oven to cook dinner for the family.
• Carol turns the computer system on when she gets to work.
• The family sits down together to watch their favourite soap on TV.
• Bethan gets home to find that the house is dark.
• Carol makes Bryn have a bath before he goes to bed.
• The Jones' night storage heater comes on automatically.

C Events in a weekday in the life of the Jones family – parents Carol and David, and teenage children Bethan and Bryn

Activities

1 Look at sources A, B and C.
  a) When is the most likely time of day for people to boil a kettle? Find this time on graph A. What do you notice? How do you explain it?
  b) Read the events in box C. At what time of day is each one likely to happen?
  c) On a copy of graph A, mark each event on the line at the correct point.
  d) Account for the shape of the line on the graph.

2 a) Draw a similar graph to show how energy demand would change during a typical **weekend** day during winter. How might the pattern differ from a weekday?
  b) Label the line on the graph with events from your family's life.

Homework

3 Find out how much electricity your family uses during a typical day. Your teacher will give you a sheet to help you.

... and supply

Britain is fortunate to have many natural sources of energy. Since the Industrial Revolution until recently, Britain has relied mainly on coal mined from coalfields in different parts of the country. But since about 1970 the oil and gas fields, discovered off-shore in the North Sea, have been **exploited**. During this time the importance of coal as a source of energy has declined, as graph D shows.

North Sea gas is now used in most homes and competes with coal as the most important fuel burned in power stations. Both oil and gas are drilled from rock beneath the sea and are piped ashore. Oil is **refined** and separated into different oil products at oil refineries on the coast.

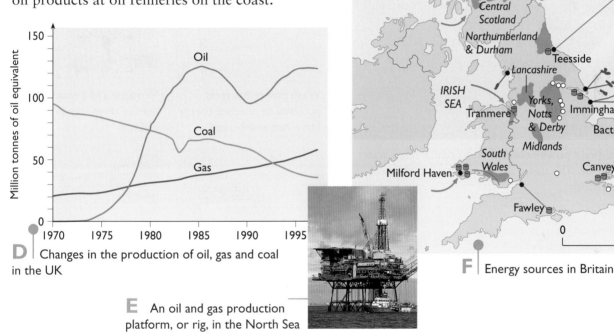

D | Changes in the production of oil, gas and coal in the UK

F | Energy sources in Britain

E | An oil and gas production platform, or rig, in the North Sea

---

4 Look at graph D.
  a) Describe the changes in the production of oil, gas and coal since 1970.
  b) Describe the effect on the graph of:
    i) the discovery of North Sea oil in about 1970
    ii) the closure of coal mines since the 1980s.

5 Look at map F.
  a) Describe the distribution of the three main energy sources – coal, oil and gas – in and around Britain.
  b) Explain the location on the map of:
    i) coal-fired power stations
    ii) oil refineries.

6 The diagram below shows how we obtain energy from gas.

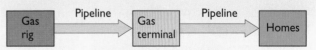

Draw two similar diagrams to show how we obtain energy from oil and coal. Choose the correct words from the box for your diagrams.

> power station   refinery   transmission line
> coal mine   tanker lorry   pipeline   oil rig   train

4.3

Renewable and non-renewable resources

The resources that can provide energy can be grouped into two main types.

- **Non-renewable resources** can be used only once because they are burnt to provide energy. Fossil fuels, like coal, are non-renewable and are gradually being **depleted** (used up). Once they have been used they cannot be replaced.

- **Renewable resources** can be used over and over again without being used up. Sunshine, wind and waves are renewable because they will never run out. They also have the advantage that, as they are not burnt, they don't cause air pollution.

A A **coal-fired power station** burns coal. It heats water to produce steam. The steam is used to drive a **turbine** to generate electricity.

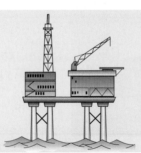

Oil is drilled from rocks beneath land or sea. It is used mainly for road transport and is the world's main source of energy

B A **hydro-electric power** station. Fast-flowing water is used to turn the turbines. These generate electricity. Water is often collected behind a dam in deep valleys.

Wave power has great potential to produce energy, but is not widely used

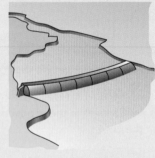

Wood is still a major source of energy in some LEDCs

Solar power is a growing source of energy in sunny parts of the world

Tidal power can be harnessed in river estuaries, but is not widely used

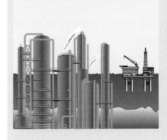

Natural gas, like oil, is drilled from rock. It can be burnt to provide heat or to generate electricity

Geothermal power comes from heat deep within the Earth. It is used in countries where there is volcanic activity

C

Both renewable and non-renewable resources can be used to produce electricity. Less than two per cent of energy used in Britain comes from renewable sources. The government has said that it wants to increase this to ten per cent by the year 2020. This would help to reduce air pollution and to conserve non-renewable sources, like coal, oil and gas. But most UK power stations can only produce electricity from fossil fuels, which are non-renewable.

D A **wind farm**. Wind drives the turbines to generate electricity. Wind farms are a common sight on coasts and hills in Britain.

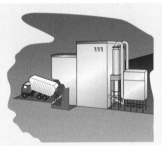

Waste can be burnt to produce energy. This is an efficient way to produce electricity in cities.

E A **nuclear power** station uses nuclear fuel, like uranium, rather than fossil fuel to produce heat. It needs large volumes of water for cooling and creates dangerous radioactive waste.

Activities

1 Study these two pages, which show different resources that provide energy.

Sort the resources into two groups: non-renewable and renewable. Complete a table showing the two groups.

2 Look at photos A, B, D and E.
   a) Choose the best site on the island below to locate each type of power station.
   b) Give two reasons for choosing each site.

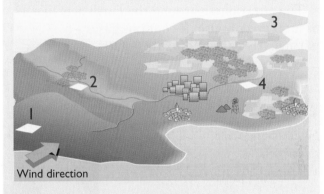

Wind direction

3 Read the newspaper headlines below.
   a) Match each headline to one of the energy resources on these two pages.
   b) In each case, explain the link between the headline and the energy resource.
   c) Of all the energy resources, which is likely to do least damage to the environment? Give reasons.

> **Soil erosion a problem as forests disappear**

> **Villages drowned for new power scheme**

> **Tanker spill threatens coastal wildlife**

> **Residents blame health problems on radiation**

4 Work in groups of three.
   Find each of the following countries in an atlas: Iceland, Australia, Denmark.
   a) Use the atlas to each find out about the climate, natural resources and volcanic activity in one country. Share your information with your group.
   b) Together, choose one renewable resource that could be developed to provide energy in each country. Give reasons for your choice.

FRAMEWORK

4.4 Global warming

Have you heard that the Earth's climate is getting warmer? It may not feel like it to you, but the average temperature around the world has increased by 1 °C over the past five hundred years. Half of this increase happened during the past hundred years. Most of the warmest years in the twentieth century were in the 1990s. Scientists have linked this **global warming** with the amount of energy that we use.

The atmosphere around the Earth acts like a natural greenhouse. It contains gases – particularly carbon dioxide (CO_2) – that allow rays from the Sun to pass through and to warm up the Earth's surface. However, these gases also trap some of the heat that the Earth gives off so that it is unable to escape. This is the **greenhouse effect**. Without it the Earth would either boil or freeze.

As we burn fossil fuels the amount of CO_2 and other gases in the atmosphere increases. More heat is trapped and the temperature goes up. One degree may not sound like much, but if this process continues it could have disastrous consequences for the world.

The remaining heat escapes through the glass, otherwise the greenhouse would overheat.

Some heat is absorbed by the glass and trapped.

The Sun's rays (short-wave radiation) pass through the glass without being absorbed. They are absorbed by the ground, heating it up.

Heat (long-wave radiation) is given off by the ground, making the greenhouse warmer.

A   The energy balance in a greenhouse

Activities

1 Look at photo A.
   a) Explain why gardeners use a greenhouse to grow plants.
   b) Compare the photo and the labels with the diagram on the right. On a large copy of the diagram, write similar labels to explain how the greenhouse effect keeps the Earth warm. Use the words atmosphere and Earth to replace glass and greenhouse.

2 a) Why is the greenhouse effect essential to life on Earth?
   b) Explain how human activities could turn the greenhouse effect into a problem.

3 Look at satellite photo B and use an atlas.
   a) Match the places labelled on the photo with the names in the box opposite.

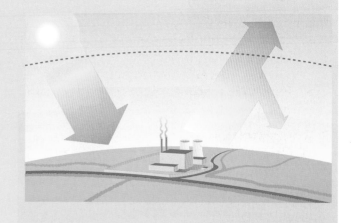

Arctic Ocean   Siberia   Bangladesh   Canada
Mediterranean Sea   The Alps   Caribbean Sea   USA
Indian Ocean   Sahara Desert

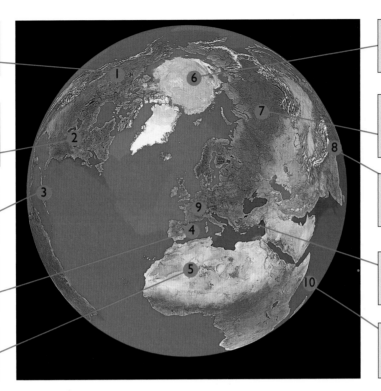

Forests damaged by heat and drought

Crop areas move north as climate warms

Increase in number of storms

Beaches disappear as sea level rises

Desert advances north to replace crops

Ice melts, making sea level rise

Frozen ground melts, damaging roads and pipelines

River delta flooded by sea

Ski resorts close due to lack of snow

Islands disappear below sea

B Scientists have predicted the impact of global warming on different parts of the world.

b) Complete a table listing the effects that global warming could have in each of these places according to photo B.
c) Explain how global warming could lead to a rise in sea level.
d) Name ten major cities around the world that could disappear if the sea level rose.

4 Look at graph C.
   a) Describe how global temperature and carbon **emissions** (the amount of CO_2 released into the atmosphere) have changed since 1860.
   b) Explain the connection between the two lines on the graph.

5 Look at photo D.
   a) Describe two ways in which burning trees adds to the greenhouse effect.
   b) Write a letter to the government in Brazil to explain why you are worried about deforestation.

6 Now, can you solve the mystery in activity 5 on page 69? How could energy conservation help save polar bears? Your teacher may give you a sheet to help you to work it out.

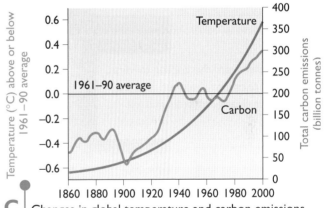

C Changes in global temperature and carbon emissions

D Deforestation in Brazil. Trees take CO_2 from the air and replace it with oxygen.

In this Building Block you will investigate two energy sources in Britain and consider the best option for the future.

4.5

Is any source of energy perfect?

Britain has massive coal **reserves** – enough to keep making electricity for 400 years. But coal mines are being closed down and power stations are turning to other fuels. Does this sound crazy to you? Let's find out why it's happening . . .

Burning coal in power stations worldwide is one of the main contributors to global warming. A large coal-fired power station emits over three million tonnes of CO_2 into the air each year. If we continue to burn fossil fuels, like coal, at the current rate, the amount of CO_2 in the atmosphere will double by the year 2060. Global temperatures could rise by 4 °C or more.

No wonder that environmentalists and some politicians argue that we have to cut the amount of coal we burn.

But that is not the only reason we are using less coal. The other reason is cost. Gas is now a cheap alternative to coal for use in power stations. Some coal-fired power stations have been converted to take gas and new gas-fired power stations have also been built. However, it is also possible to import coal that is cheaper than the coal produced in Britain. Imported coal is now used in many power stations in Britain. So even though we are mining less, coal remains an important source of energy.

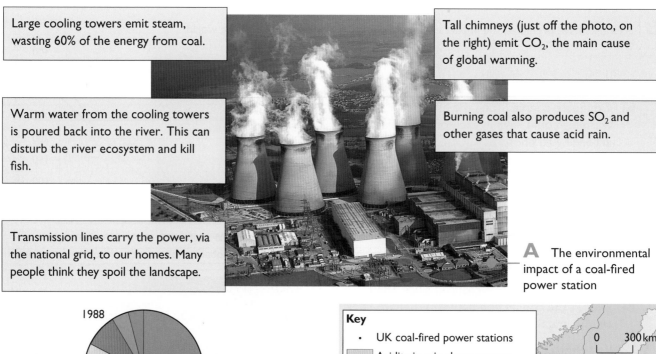

Large cooling towers emit steam, wasting 60% of the energy from coal.

Tall chimneys (just off the photo, on the right) emit CO_2, the main cause of global warming.

Warm water from the cooling towers is poured back into the river. This can disturb the river ecosystem and kill fish.

Burning coal also produces SO_2 and other gases that cause acid rain.

Transmission lines carry the power, via the national grid, to our homes. Many people think they spoil the landscape.

A   The environmental impact of a coal-fired power station

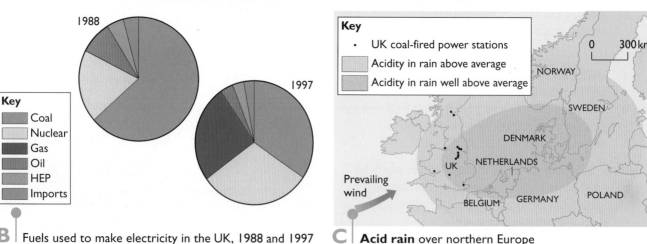

1988

1997

Key
- Coal
- Nuclear
- Gas
- Oil
- HEP
- Imports

Key
- • UK coal-fired power stations
- Acidity in rain above average
- Acidity in rain well above average

0   300 km

NORWAY

SWEDEN

DENMARK

NETHERLANDS

UK

Prevailing wind

BELGIUM   GERMANY   POLAND

B | Fuels used to make electricity in the UK, 1988 and 1997

C | **Acid rain** over northern Europe

I am one of a dying breed. Coal-mining once sustained hundreds of communities all over Britain, from Kent to Lancashire, South Wales to Scotland. Now there are precious few mines left. Closing the mines has caused untold misery in those communities. It's led to unemployment, poverty, broken families – you name it.

I think that closing the mines is madness – what a waste of resources! In years to come they'll wish they'd never done it. Once the mines are closed they will flood, and it will cost ten times more to get the coal out then.

D A coalminer at Selby, Yorkshire – one of Britain's few remaining deep mines

The only part of the coal industry in Britain that has grown in recent years is **open-cast mining**. This employs fewer people than deep mining, making it cheaper. Giant earth-scrapers remove the overlying soil and rock until they reach the layers of coal beneath. This creates major scars on the landscape. After the coal is extracted, the landscape is restored to something like its former state.

E An open-cast mine near Chesterfield in Derbyshire

Activities

1 Look at photo A, which shows a power station at Drax in Yorkshire.
   a) Make two lists of the effects that a coal-fired power station has on the environment:
       i) local effects   ii) global effects.
   b) Explain how the following people might be affected by coal-fired power stations in Britain:

   • a resident in the village of Drax
   • a forest manager in Sweden
   • an inhabitant of the Maldives (islands in the Indian Ocean).

2 Look at the pie charts in B.
   a) Estimate the percentage of each type of fuel used in 1988 and in 1997. Describe the changes that happened.
   b) How can you explain any of these changes?

3 Look at map C.
   a) Describe the pattern of the level of acidity in rainfall across Europe.

	1973	1997
Total coal production (million tonnes)	132	48.6
Deep mine production (mt)	121.9	31.9
Open-cast mine production (mt)	10.1	16.7
Number of employees	252,000	17,300
Number of deep mines	259	22

F Changes in coal production in Britain

   b) What evidence does the map provide that power stations in the UK cause acid rain in Norway and Sweden?

4 Look at table F.
   a) Draw suitable graphs to illustrate the data in the table.
   b) Explain why these changes have happened.
   c) Study sources D and E. Describe the impact that the changes in the coal industry have had on:
       i) the environment   ii) mining communities.

As free as the wind?

Britain is a windy island. It is one of the windiest countries in Europe. Yet although wind power is now the fastest growing form of renewable energy in Britain, it still produces only a tiny fraction of our total energy. The first British wind farm was not built until 1990.

One of the main attractions of wind power is that it produces no air pollution, so it does not contribute to global warming. However, people say wind farms spoil the landscape and those living nearby complain about the noise of the turbines.

G The Yorkshire moors inspired the book *Wuthering Heights* by Emily Brontë.

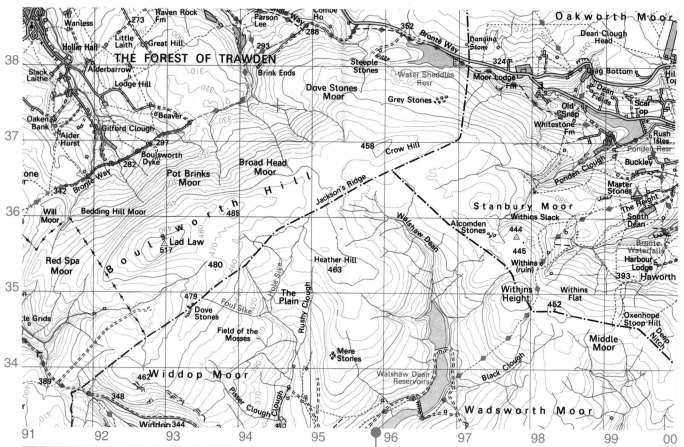

H The Yorkshire moors. Reproduced from the 1998 1:50,000 Ordnance Survey map by permission of the Controller of HMSO © Crown Copyright

Criteria for choosing a wind farm site:

- average wind speed of no less than 5 metres per second throughout the year
- an exposed site, open to the prevailing westerly wind
- gently sloping land or plateau – steep land causes too much wind turbulence
- away from forest or buildings that reduce wind speed and increase turbulence
- outside protected areas, like national parks, where planning permission may not be given.

Site	Slope	Direction facing	Wind speed (m/second)		
			Average	Max.	Min.
1	steep	south-east	12	40	5
2	gentle	south-west	18	45	10
3	very steep	south	8	20	0
4	gentle	hilltop	19	50	10

I Britain's largest wind farm at Llandinam in Wales

J Sir Bernard Ingham, a prominent campaigner against wind farms

> Forests of these infernal contraptions are springing up on our pristine Pennine moors. Yet wind power is no such thing. Each turbine generates but a tiny fraction – one thousandth or less – of the electricity from a small power station. It is unreliable even in a blowy winter.

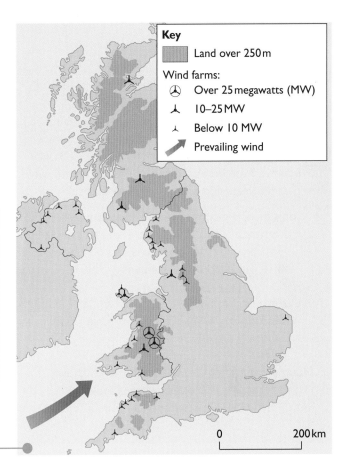

Key

▨ Land over 250 m

Wind farms:
- Over 25 megawatts (MW)
- 10–25 MW
- Below 10 MW
- → Prevailing wind

0   200 km

K   Wind farms in the UK

Activities

1 Look at map H.
  a) Read the criteria for choosing a wind farm site. Find the four possible sites for a wind farm at the following grid references: 978 350, 987 377, 937 354, 962 343.

  b) Study the recordings in the table taken at each site. From the slope and direction it faces, match each site with a grid reference.

  c) Using the criteria and the recordings, choose the best site for a wind farm. Give reasons.

2 Look at photos G and I.
  a) What impact has the wind farm had on the landscape in photo I?

  b) Suggest why a planning application for a wind farm at the site in photo G was rejected.

  c) Do you think this was right? Give reasons.

3 Look at map K.
  a) Describe the distribution of wind farms in the UK.

  b) Explain this distribution in relation to:
    i) the prevailing wind
    ii) distance from the coast
    iii) land over 250 metres.

4 Will we allow a wind farm?
  a) Work in a group.
    There has been an application to build a wind farm at site 4 on map H. Prepare a case for *or* against building the wind farm here. Think of all the arguments you can to support your case.

  b) With the whole class, hold a planning committee meeting to decide whether to approve the application to build a wind farm.
    Choose a chairperson or ask your teacher to chair the meeting of the planning committee. Representatives of each group should present their case to the meeting.
    At the end, take a vote to decide whether the wind farm can be built.

  c) Write a letter to the chairperson of the meeting expressing your own view about the decision that was taken.

Assignment

Coal or wind?

The British government has said that by the year 2020 ten per cent of our electricity must come from renewable sources. Less than one per cent of our electricity currently comes from wind power, but this is increasing rapidly. About 35 per cent of our electricity now comes from burning coal, but this has halved over the past ten years and is likely to fall further still.

1 Consider the advantages and disadvantages of the two forms of energy. Use the information in this Building Block, including boxes L and M below. Think about each of the following criteria:

> cost employment space reliability
> visual impact efficiency (lack of waste)
> location pollution energy output

Complete a table like the one here to show the advantages and disadvantages under each criterion. One is done for you.

2 Is the government right to switch from non-renewable to renewable energy? Should it aim for more than ten per cent to be coming from renewable sources by 2020? Or should we stick with coal that, after all, has supplied our needs for the past hundred years?

Write a report for the government to advise them how much energy should come from wind (renewable) and coal (non-renewable) sources by the year 2020. Include in your report:

a) your table of advantages and disadvantages

b) a map of Britain to show the location of new and existing power stations and wind farms.

| | Coal | | Wind | |
	Advantages	Disadvantages	Advantages	Disadvantages
Cost	Lower cost – 0.03 p/kWh			Higher cost – 0.04–0.05 p/kWh

L | A typical coal-fired power station

Area:	120 hectares
Inputs:	9,500 tonnes of coal per day
	30 cubic metres of water per second for cooling
Structure:	one chimney 180 metres high four cooling towers each 110 metres high
Energy output:	1,000 megawatts of electricity (enough for an urban area of 750,000 people)
Other outputs:	1,350 tonnes of ash per day
	3 million tonnes of CO_2 per year
	6,500 tonnes of SO_2 per year
	60 per cent of the energy in coal is given off as heat
Cost:	0.03p per kilowatt-hour

Area:	100 hectares (most of the land can still be used for livestock grazing)
Inputs:	none
Structure:	24 wind turbines each 25 metres high
Energy output:	10 megawatts of electricity (enough for a small town of 7,500 people)
Other outputs:	noise
Cost:	0.04–0.05p per kilowatt-hour

M | A typical wind farm

In this Building Block you will investigate the USA's dependence on energy and consider the real cost of using cars.
This will also help you with the USA investigation on page 107.

4.6

The American dream, or environmental nightmare?

The United States uses more energy than any other country. The average North American uses the equivalent of 7.5 tonnes of oil every year – twice as much as the average European and over twenty times more than a person in Africa.

Like Britain, the USA has large reserves of fossil fuels – coal, oil and gas. Until 1950 these were enough to meet all its energy needs. But a growing proportion of the USA's energy now has to be imported to meet the ever increasing demand (see graph B). As oil and gas reserves begin to run out in future America will have to import more. Americans are becoming worried that their energy-dependent lifestyle may not last for ever.

A 'The sight of Las Vegas from a helicopter at night cannot fail to leave you gasping with admiration and despair at mankind's tenacity and silliness. What an amazing notion, to have created this massive Christmas tree in the middle of the desert – and what a waste of energy, both electric and human.'

Julie Burchill, controversial, outspoken journalist

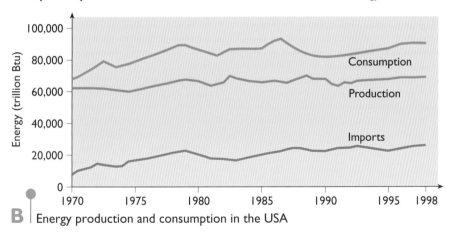

B Energy production and consumption in the USA

C The USA at night showing lights. The colour-code ranges from purple (low-intensity) to white (high-intensity).

Activities

1 Look at graph B.
   a) What does the graph show about energy production and consumption in the USA?
   b) Why should this worry Americans?

2 Look at photo A and read Julie Burchill's views about Las Vegas. Do you agree with her? Why?

3 Look at satellite photo C.
   a) Compare the photo with the map of population distribution in the USA on page 108. Explain the pattern you see in the photo.
   b) Which American cities can you identify in the photo? Can you find Las Vegas? Check the names against a map in an atlas.

In the fast lane

Not every city in the USA is like Las Vegas, which consumes a vast amount of energy even by American standards. Detroit, in the north-east, is more typical. This is where the Ford Motor Company set up its first factory in 1903. Using mass production it supplied cars that, for the first time, ordinary people were able to afford. Detroit grew with the car industry. That is why it earned the nickname 'Motown' (motor city).

Of course, industry in Detroit also created a huge demand for electricity generated by coal from the nearby coalfield. During the 1980s and 1990s many car plants relocated away from the city but the region, close to the Great Lakes, still has the main concentration of car plants in the USA.

D A car plant near Detroit

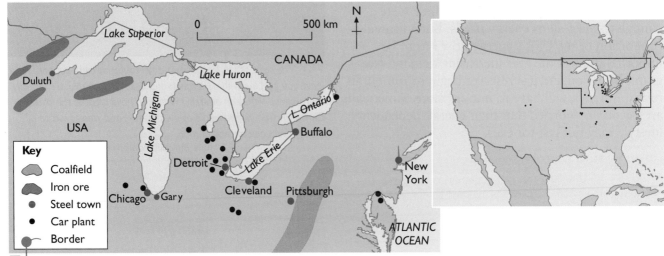

E The Great Lakes region, north-east USA, showing steel towns and car plants

Activities

1 Look at map E.
   a) Describe the distribution of steel towns in north-east USA.
   b) From the evidence on the map, suggest why they are located here. (*Clue:* think about raw materials and transport.)
   c) Describe the distribution of car plants in the region.
   d) Suggest why Detroit was a good location for the car industry. Mention power, materials, labour and markets.

2 Read source F and look at map H.
   a) i) On the map, locate each of the places that Donna mentions.
       ii) Measure the distance by road that she might drive on a typical day.

   b) Ron travels to work and back each day in his car, and also travels around the city. Estimate the total distance that the family might travel each week by car. How far would they travel in a year?

3 Look at table G.
   a) Use the data in the table to work out roughly the annual cost of car travel for the Eng family. The life expectancy of a typical car is about ten years, so add 10% of the cost of each car for a year. A typical car travels about 50 kilometres per litre of petrol in town.
   b) How does the cost of car ownership in the USA compare to the cost in the UK? How could this affect the level of car ownership and the amount of driving people do?

F The Eng family: Donna and Ron with children Christopher and Michael. Like most American families, they depend a lot on their cars.

> I work for a large American car company in Detroit. Like most people. I commute to and from work in my car. Some days I work in the office, but other days I go to meetings all over the city. Company headquarters is downtown (city centre) about 25 miles (40 km) from here. The company has spread out all over the city and beyond. I can spend a lot of time driving. I don't think I could survive in Detroit without my car. There isn't even a bus service that I could take to work.

> I make all my journeys by car. I do most of my shopping at Somerset Mall, where I get my groceries and clothes. If I need something quickly I drive to Krogers, a mile up the road. There are other shops on the strip malls along main roads, like Rochester Road.
> Sometimes I pick up the boys from school. Although it's not far, there is no sidewalk (pavement) so it's not safe to walk. When they reach sixteen we may buy them a car so that they can get to college without us having to take them.

	USA	UK
Average cost of a new car	20,000	19,200
Cost of petrol per litre	0.32	1.20
Average car insurance per year	1,200	560
Annual road tax	50–150 (varies between states)	256

G The cost of car travel in the USA and the UK (at 1999 prices, all in US $)

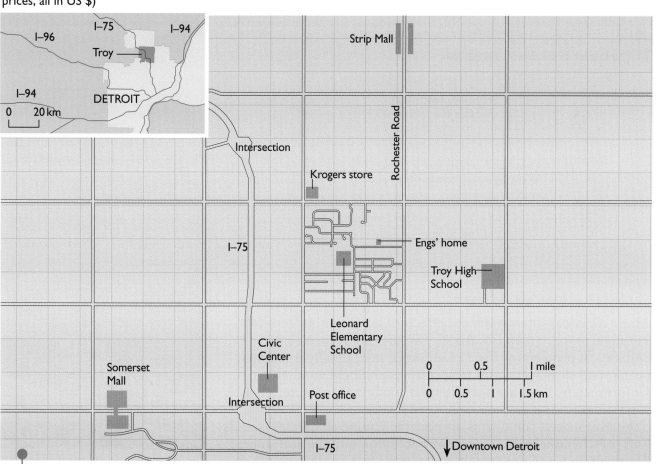

H Troy, the suburb of Detroit where the Eng family lives

Can we sustain our car culture?

The USA relies on its huge oil reserves to sustain its car culture. But as the most accessible reserves are depleted, oil exploration has been extended to more difficult environments, such as the Alaskan oilfield. This lies north of the Arctic Circle in a region that is frozen for much of the year. Oil from here has to be transported by pipeline over 1,000 kilometres across frozen land to the port of Valdez on the southern coast of Alaska. From here giant oil tankers take it to other ports in the USA.

On 24 March 1989 the tanker Exxon Valdez hit rocks close to the port, spilling its cargo of oil. The oil spread 500 kilometres along the coast causing huge damage to wildlife. Only fifteen per cent of the oil was ever recovered; even ten years later oil residues could still be found.

I The oil spill from the Exxon Valdez off the Alaskan coast

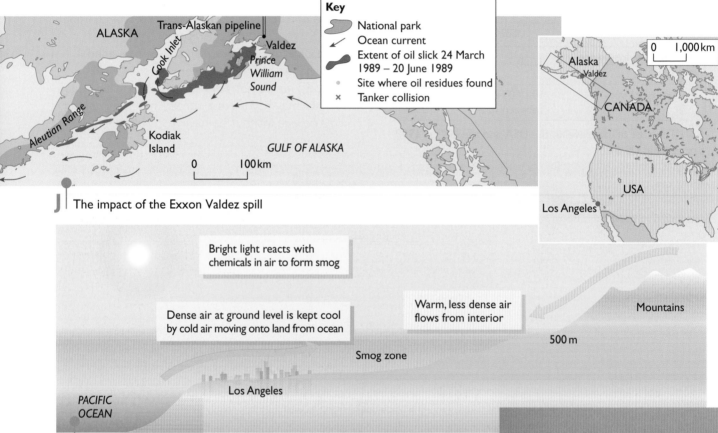

Key

National park

→ Ocean current

Extent of oil slick 24 March 1989 – 20 June 1989

• Site where oil residues found

× Tanker collision

ALASKA Trans-Alaskan pipeline Cook Inlet Valdez Prince William Sound Aleutian Range Kodiak Island GULF OF ALASKA 0 100 km

J The impact of the Exxon Valdez spill

Alaska Valdez 0 1,000 km CANADA USA Los Angeles

Bright light reacts with chemicals in air to form smog

Dense air at ground level is kept cool by cold air moving onto land from ocean

Warm, less dense air flows from interior

Mountains

500 m

Smog zone

Los Angeles

PACIFIC OCEAN

K Smog formation over Los Angeles

Many American cities suffer the effects of air pollution from cars, but none more so than Los Angeles on the Californian coast. Millions of people now live in California, attracted by its climate – year-round sunshine, warm temperatures and light winds. Unfortunately, these are also the ideal conditions for smog formation.

In most places, sun warms air near the ground so that it expands and rises. This helps to disperse any pollution into the atmosphere. However, in Los Angeles, cold ocean currents keep the surface air cool so that it does not rise and escape, trapping pollution from cars.

L A busy freeway in Los Angeles – one of the sources of pollution

M | Chief executive of a US car company

The car industry is doing all it can to respond to environmental problems. Our cars are now cleaner and more fuel-efficient than ever before. They can travel over twice the number of kilometres to the litre than they did in 1974. And they emit fifteen per cent less carbon dioxide than they did in 1987. But our customers keep demanding larger vehicles, more powerful engines and more luxury features. The challenge is to meet these demands while, at the same time, making our cars more environmentally friendly.

Greenpeace is not against cars. But we believe that the government must do all it can to encourage people to reduce car use. It can do this by providing better public transport. Cities need to be planned that allow people to walk or cycle and avoid the need for cars. The government should also promote renewable sources of energy such as solar, wind and wave power to reduce our dependence on non-renewable sources.

N | An environmentalist working with Greenpeace, USA

Activities

1 Look at photo I and map J.
  a) Suggest why oil has to be transported by pipeline across Alaska before it is taken by tanker.
  b) Describe the spread of oil after the tanker collided. Using map J, explain why it spread in this way.
  c) What environmental damage could have been caused?

2 Look at diagram K and photo L.
  a) Explain how smog is formed in Los Angeles.
  b) Why is it worse than in other US cities?

3 a) Explain how both the Exxon Valdez disaster and smog in Los Angeles are connected with cars.
  b) Think of other environmental problems linked to cars.

Assignment

What is the real cost of driving a car?

Some environmentalists suggest that a 'carbon tax' should be added to the price of petrol. The money raised could be used to pay for better public transport and reduce the need for cars. The theory is that as car travel becomes more expensive, drivers think more carefully before journeys and they tend to drive less.

How much should drivers pay for a litre of petrol? You are going to write a report for the US government, recommending how much to charge.

1 Consider each of the environmental costs of cars in the box below. Rank them in order of importance with the one that concerns you most first.

noise   road congestion   oil pollution   smog   road building   accidents
car parking   acid rain   global warming   resource depletion

2 In the USA the price of a litre of petrol in 1999 was $0.32c. For each environmental cost, how much tax should be added to the cost of a litre of petrol? The greater the cost, the more tax could be added. In each case give a reason to support your decision.

3 a) Work out the total price you would charge for a litre of petrol.
  b) Explain the effect this might have on the number of cars and how much people drive them.
  c) Finally, suggest how you would use the money you raise from tax.

DIGGING DEEPER

4.7

Can we get out of the greenhouse?

Do you think of yourself as a gas-guzzler? One-quarter of the world's population, living in MEDCs (and that includes you!), consumes 70 per cent of the world's energy. The remaining three-quarters of the world's population, in LEDCs, consumes just 30 per cent of the world's energy.

The amount of energy that the world uses is expected to double between 1996 and 2020. Much of the rise will come in LEDCs where population is growing faster than in MEDCs, and lifestyles are changing faster. As these countries industrialise and people migrate from rural areas to cities, so energy consumption increases.

The problem is that the rate at which fossil fuels are being burned is unsustainable. Just at the time when people in MEDCs have realised they need to reduce energy consumption, people in LEDCs need to use more.

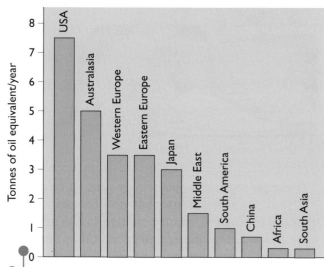

A Energy consumption per capita around the world
Source: Adapted from *BP Amoco Statistical Review of World Energy*

	World population (%)	World energy consumption (%)
Africa	9	3
Asia	60	18
Australasia	1	2
Europe	16	44
North America	5	28
South America	9	5

B Population and energy consumption by continent

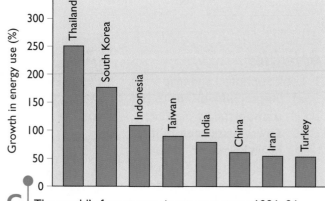

C The world's fastest growing energy users 1986–96
Source: Adapted from *BP Amoco Statistical Review of World Energy*

D Women in Cameroon in Africa collecting wood, the main source of energy in rural areas

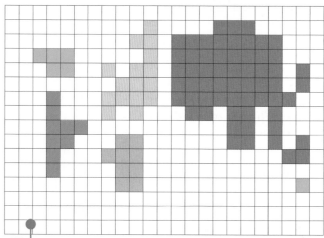

E Map showing the world's population, using figures in table B. Each square represents one per cent of the total population.

The governments of most countries now accept what some scientists have been saying for many years: that global warming is a result of burning fossil fuels. At the present rate of increase, it is predicted that average world temperatures will increase by as much as 3–4 °C by the year 2100, enough to cause massive disruption to the world's climate.

But politicians find it hard to take the action necessary to cut energy consumption to safer levels. This would mean making unpopular decisions that would dramatically affect people's lifestyle.

At an important meeting held in Kyoto, Japan, in 1997, leaders of the world's richest countries reluctantly agreed targets to reduce the burning of fossil fuels in their countries.

KYOTO DEAL 'LEAVES USA FREE TO POLLUTE'

Emission targets agreed at Kyoto for 2012 (percentage of 1990 levels)	
Iceland	110
Australia	108
Norway	101
New Zealand, Russia, Ukraine	100
Croatia	95
Canada, Hungary, Japan, Poland	94
USA	93
All other European countries	92

It was the longest night of the most bad-tempered negotiations in which 160 governments have ever engaged. In the end, they emerged with an agreement that may cut global greenhouse gas emissions by an average 5.2% by the year 2012.

But in the USA the new treaty may be voted down as Congress members representing coal, oil and steel interests vote it out. US vice-president, Al Gore, claimed, 'It is a vital turning point in the global warming fight,' but a spokesperson for Greenpeace said, 'It is a tragedy and a farce.'

The agreement requires that the European Union, the USA and Japan reduce their greenhouse emissions to below 1990 levels. In all, 38 of the world's richest countries will cut emissions below 1990 levels, but Russia, Ukraine and LEDCs do not have to make any reduction. Australia, Iceland and Norway, already committed to new energy projects, will be allowed to increase their levels.

The US failed to achieve all its aims, which included making the LEDCs also agree to targets. But the US itself could avoid making any cuts by trading their carbon emissions with countries that manage to reduce their emissions by more than required. EU commissioner Ritt Bjerregaard remained doubtful. 'This is not good enough for the future,' she said. 'We would have liked countries to be more ambitious. But with pressure from the car manufacturers and the oil companies I think it was encouraging that we came up with a deal at all.'

F Extract adapted from the *Guardian*, 12 December 1997

Activities

1 Look at graphs A and C.
   a) From graph A, how much greater is energy consumption in the US than in other parts of the world?
   b) From graph C, suggest how the pattern of energy consumption around the world may change in future.

2 Look at table B and map E.
   a) On a similar grid to map E, draw a map to show energy consumption for each continent using figures from table B. Try to make the shapes look like the real continents.
   b) Compare your map with map E. Describe what they show.

3 Read extract F. Answer the questions.
   a) Why do you think it was so hard for the governments to reach an agreement?
   b) What pressure was there on the US government not to agree reductions?

   c) Would it be reasonable to expect LEDCs to try to reduce their energy use? Give reasons.
   d) Why do you think that Greenpeace described the deal as 'a tragedy and a farce'?
   e) Imagine that you are one of the women in photo D. What would you think of the Kyoto agreement?

4 Work with a small group. Some of you could represent MEDCs and others LEDCs. Produce your own agreement on energy consumption around the world.

   Think about each of the questions below as you come to your agreement:

   • Should the world try to cut the use of fossil fuels? What changes in lifestyle should people be forced to make?
   • Should all countries share equal responsibility, or should some take more than others?
   • Should any countries be allowed to increase their use of fossil fuels? If so, which ones?

DIGGING DEEPER

What can we learn from the poor?

Not everybody in the world aspires to the energy-hungry lifestyle of people in the world's richest countries. In any case, many people now recognise that this lifestyle is not sustainable.

However, there are alternatives. It may be that we, living in a rich MEDC, can learn from LEDCs. People living in these poorer countries have learnt to live using less energy and making better use of renewable sources of energy that are widely available. Boxes G and H below show just two of the possibilities we could learn from.

People in the mountains of Nepal have added a new feature to their homes. They now have photovoltaic cells that allow them to capture solar energy. Solar panels are well adapted to an isolated rural lifestyle, since they can be set up and function anywhere.

The cells work even when the sun doesn't shine, particularly when there is snow to reflect the natural light. A single 40–60 watt solar module provides a family with five hours' light, four hours' TV or fifteen hours of radio per day. The Nepalese government hopes that renewable energy will bring electricity to rural areas and slow down migration to the city.

G

H

People in Indian villages use their waste to provide light and warmth. In the state of Karnataka, few people could afford the electricity from the state grid. Biogas plants are communally-owned and provide electricity for everyone.

The biogas plant digests dung and agricultural waste to produce a gas – 60% methane, 40% CO_2 – that is used to fuel engines and generate electricity. This goes to people's homes and is also used to pump water around the village, so making life easier for the village women. Biogas plants are now common in villages around India.

Assignment

What can you do about global warming?

You have been asked by the government to devise an alternative energy plan for your local community or, perhaps, your school. This should contribute to the government's commitment to reduce emissions of greenhouse gases.

1 Think of all the ways in which energy is wasted. This could include all forms of energy: electricity, petrol in cars, and even the rubbish people throw away.

2 Think about the potential for using renewable forms of energy locally. This will depend on where you live – urban or rural, sunny or windy.

3 Produce an energy plan that includes ideas for both energy conservation and energy production.

In the USA people bring water hundreds of kilometres from the nearest river so that they can grow crops in the desert.

In Britain, we take water for granted, but without water life as we know it would be impossible. Water is essential in our households, for our health, for industry and for agriculture.

- How do people obtain water in the places shown in each of these photos?
- How might this affect the way that water is used in each place?
- How do you use water in your home?
- In what other ways do people in more economically developed countries depend on water?

In rural Bangladesh people collect water from the village well.

GROUNDWORK

5.1

How much water do you use?

We are surrounded by water: in the sea, in the air, in rivers and lakes and even below the ground. In Britain – particularly when the weather is wet – there seems to be more water than we really need! So, you might wonder, why do we have to pay for it?

Although water is a freely available resource, it still has to be stored, purified, piped to our homes, and then cleaned and **recycled** after we have used it. All this costs money – and there are environmental costs too. Water is stored in **reservoirs** that take up land. Many human activities can cause water pollution. Only during a **drought**, when water is scarce, do we realise what a valuable resource our water is.

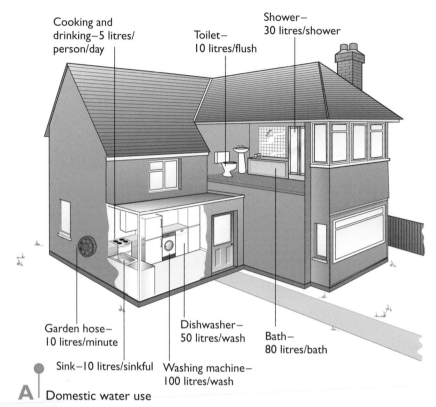

Cooking and drinking–5 litres/person/day

Toilet–10 litres/flush

Shower–30 litres/shower

Garden hose–10 litres/minute

Dishwasher–50 litres/wash

Bath–80 litres/bath

Sink–10 litres/sinkful

Washing machine–100 litres/wash

A Domestic water use

B A garden sprinkler is one of the heaviest domestic users of water.

Key
- Personal washing
- Cooking and drinking
- Laundry
- Washing dishes
- Watering garden
- Washing car
- Flushing toilet
- Other

Bangladesh – most people live in villages and collect water from a well or borehole

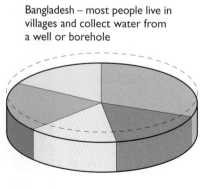

UK – most people live in cities. Water is piped to people's homes

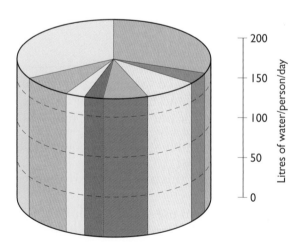

Litres of water/person/day

200
150
100
50
0

C Water consumption in Bangladesh and the UK

10 AUGUST 1995

YORKSHIRE WATER LEVELS REACH CRISIS POINT

As Britain scorches in temperatures over 30 °C Yorkshire Water yesterday warned people to use less water. Already there is a hosepipe ban to stop people watering gardens or cleaning cars. But water levels in local reservoirs are now dangerously low. The company fears it may have to turn off supplies to homes.

People could be forced to collect water from standpipes in the street. One old lady in Bradford asked, 'How do they expect me to collect water in a bucket at my age? It wasn't this bad in the war.'

A spokeswoman from Yorkshire Water explained, 'Either people need to use less water or else we had better start praying for rain.'

D Extract adapted from the *West Yorkshire Gazette*

Water shortages, caused by drought, show how important it is to conserve the water we have. This is something that we can all help to do. Water companies, like Yorkshire Water, encourage people to reduce the amount of water that they use by installing water meters. With a meter you only pay for the water you use, like gas or electricity. People tend to use less water if they know they are paying for it. Most new homes these days have a water meter.

Activities

1 Look at drawing A.
   a) Work out how much water your family might use today.
   b) Suggest what differences there may be between the amount of water used in summer and in winter. Give reasons.

2 Look at diagram C.
   a) Using the scale, work out the total daily water consumption for a Bangladeshi villager and a British city-dweller.
   b) Estimate the percentage of water used for different purposes by each person.
   c) What does this tell you about the different ways water is used in MEDCs and LEDCs?

3 Read extract D.
   a) When did this drought happen? Explain why droughts are more likely to happen at this time of year in Britain.
   b) What happens to water consumption at this time of year? Explain why water shortages are most likely to happen then.
   c) Imagine that you work for a water company. What advice would you give to your customers to conserve water:
      i) in the short term
      ii) in the long term?

Homework

4 a) Find out how much your family's water bill is each year.
   b) Is your water metered? If it is not metered, work out how much you would pay if it was. Your teacher will give you a sheet to help you to do this.
   c) Think of ways in which your family could conserve water. (If your water is metered this could also save you money.)

FRAMEWORK

5.2 Water supply in Britain

Our water comes from two main sources: **surface water**, found in lakes and rivers, and **groundwater** that collects below ground level in rock. Together, these two sources make up less than one per cent of all the world's water. Ninety-seven per cent is stored in the oceans and two per cent is locked up as ice near the North and South Poles (see diagram A).

Surface water is usually found above impermeable rock, which does not allow water to pass through. Groundwater is found in permeable rock, beneath the level of the **water table**. However, when permeable rock is saturated, the water table comes to the surface and may form a **spring**, where water flows naturally from the ground. Traditionally, people in Britain obtained water from rivers and springs, or by sinking wells to reach groundwater. Most settlements first grew at sites where water was easily obtained.

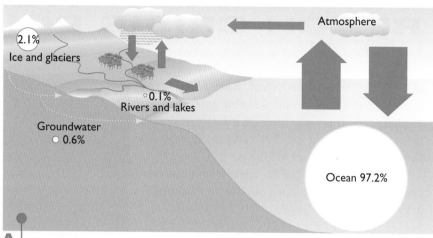

2.1% Ice and glaciers

0.1% Rivers and lakes

Groundwater 0.6%

Atmosphere

Ocean 97.2%

A The world's water stores

Unfortunately, in Britain today water is not always found in the areas where it is most needed. The greatest demand for water is in the South-east of England, the area where most people live. However, much of our water supply comes from the North-west, which receives the greatest rainfall. Water is stored here in lakes or reservoirs before it is transferred by pipe or by river to cities where it is needed.

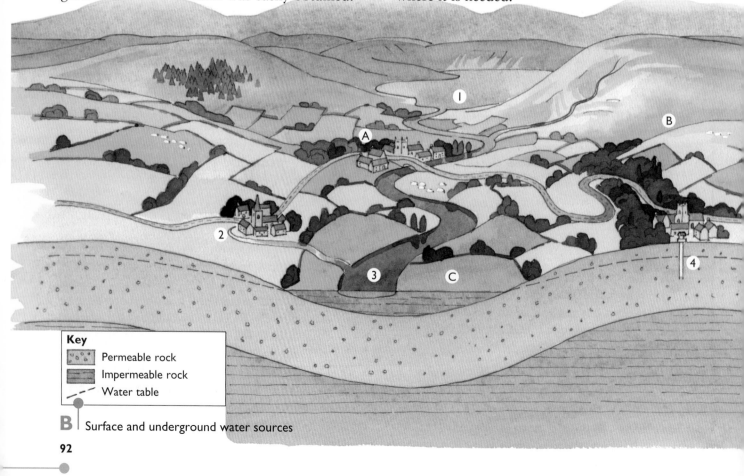

Key

Permeable rock

Impermeable rock

Water table

B Surface and underground water sources

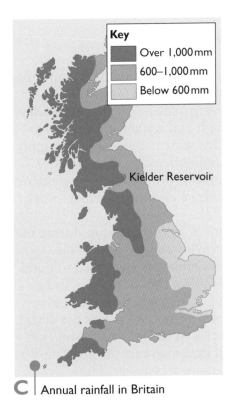

Key
- Over 1,000 mm
- 600–1,000 mm
- Below 600 mm

Kielder Reservoir

C Annual rainfall in Britain

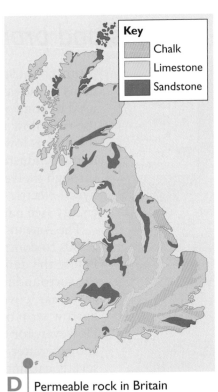

Key
- Chalk
- Limestone
- Sandstone

D Permeable rock in Britain

North of Scotland

West of Scotland   East of Scotland

Northumbrian

North West   Yorkshire

Severn–Trent

Anglian

Dwr Cymru   Thames

South West   Southern

Wessex

E Water companies in Britain

Activities

1 Look at diagram A.
   a) Describe how the water cycle works.
      Mention each of these processes in your
      description: *evaporation, condensation,
      precipitation, run-off.*
   b) Which water stores are usually used to supply
      water and which are not? Explain why.

2 Look at drawing B.
   a) Match the numbers on the drawing with the
      following water sources: *a river, a well, a
      spring, a lake.*

   b) Suggest which of these sources might provide:
      i) the cleanest
      ii) the most reliable
      supply of water. Give reasons.
   c) Which site on the drawing – A, B or C –
      would be the best place to make a reservoir?
      Give reasons.

3 Look at maps C, D and E and photo F.
   a) Suggest three reasons why Kielder was a
      good site for a reservoir.
   b) Chalk, limestone and sandstone are all
      permeable rocks. From maps D and E, name
      three water companies most likely to supply
      at least some of their water from
      groundwater sources. Explain why.

Homework

4 Which water company supplies water to your home?
   Find out exactly where your water supply
   comes from. What happens to the water before it
   reaches your home? What happens to it after it
   leaves your home?

   ICT You could use the Internet to obtain
   information from your local water company's
   website.

F Kielder Reservoir in Northumbria is the largest
reservoir in Britain.

5.3

Dam-building – benefits and problems

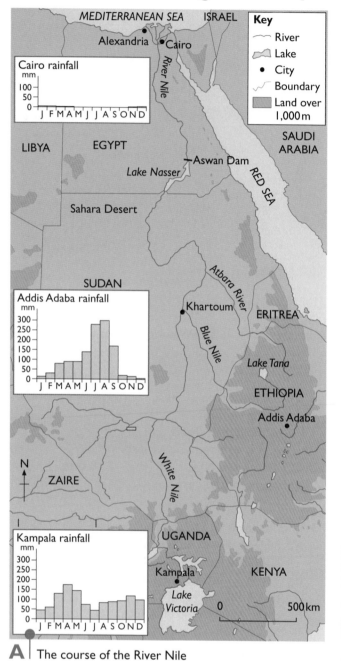

A | The course of the River Nile

Many countries around the world have built huge **dams** to tackle their water problems. Dams are used to control rivers: reducing flood levels when the river flow is high and releasing water when the flow is low. This water can be used to supply homes, industry and agriculture with water through the year. Dams are also used to generate hydro-electric power, a clean, renewable form of energy (see page 72).

The Aswan Dam in Egypt was built during the 1960s to control the flow of the River Nile. Before the dam was built, the river used to flood the surrounding land for two or three months each year, covering it with **silt**. This created a narrow strip of fertile farmland across the desert. However, for the rest of the year there was not enough water and in some years the flooding was severe, causing damage to villages. The government built the Aswan Dam to ensure a reliable water supply throughout the year. Much of the water was used to provide **irrigation** to help farmers to grow more crops. But, although the dam solved some problems, it created several new ones.

B | The Aswan Dam

Activities

1 Look at map A.
   a) Name the countries through which the Nile and its tributaries flow.
   b) Use the scale to measure the length of the Nile from the source of the White Nile to the Mediterranean.

2 Look at the three rainfall graphs on the map and find the three places.

a) Describe the annual rainfall pattern in each place.

b) For much of its course the Nile flows through desert. Explain where the water comes from.

c) Before the Aswan Dam was built, the river flooded each year from May to July. Explain why this happened.

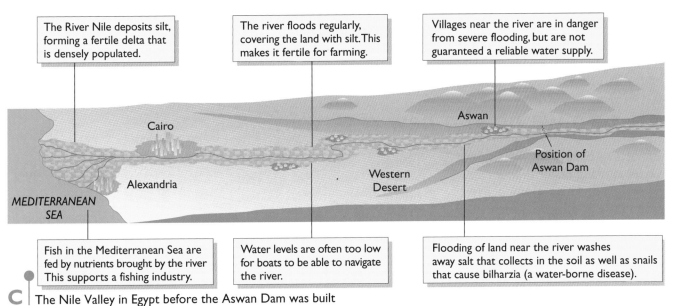

The River Nile deposits silt, forming a fertile delta that is densely populated.

The river floods regularly, covering the land with silt. This makes it fertile for farming.

Villages near the river are in danger from severe flooding, but are not guaranteed a reliable water supply.

Aswan

Cairo

Position of Aswan Dam

Western Desert

Alexandria

MEDITERRANEAN SEA

Fish in the Mediterranean Sea are fed by nutrients brought by the river This supports a fishing industry.

Water levels are often too low for boats to be able to navigate the river.

Flooding of land near the river washes away salt that collects in the soil as well as snails that cause bilharzia (a water-borne disease).

C | The Nile Valley in Egypt before the Aswan Dam was built

The Mediterranean fishing industry has declined.

Electricity provides power for industry and homes.

More people suffer from bilharzia.

Boats sail up and down the Nile all through the year.

Farmers have to use artificial fertiliser to grow crops.

Villages are no longer flooded.

Lake Nasser is gradually filling up with silt.

Farmers grow crops all through the year using irrigation.

The Nile delta is shrinking as the sea erodes it.

Water evaporates from the soil so it gets salty.

Towns and villages have a reliable water supply.

A new fishing industry has grown on Lake Nasser.

D | Benefits and problems brought about by the Aswan Dam

3 Look at drawing C.
  a) Complete a table listing the advantages and disadvantages that Egypt experienced from the River Nile *before* the Aswan Dam was built.
  b) On a copy of the drawing, draw the Aswan Dam with Lake Nasser in the valley behind it.

4 Read diagram D.
  a) Sort the statements into two groups: benefits and problems.

  b) Use the statements to label your drawing from activity 3b. Write benefits above the drawing and problems below it. Draw an arrow from each, pointing to the correct part of the drawing.

  c) Choose two benefits and two problems. Explain how each one can be linked to the building of the dam. For example: *the Nile delta is shrinking because silt is trapped behind the dam and is no longer being deposited at the delta.*

In this Building Block you will consider the need for a new reservoir in Oxfordshire and, if such a reservoir should be built, whether a proposed site near Abingdon is suitable.

5.4 Do we need a new reservoir?

In parts of Britain the demand for water is rising faster than it can be supplied. This is particularly true in the South-east which, as well as being the driest region, also has the fastest-growing population. Two-thirds of the region's water supply is taken from rivers, mainly the River Thames. The rest comes from groundwater stored in **aquifers** (permeable rock that lies below much of the South-east).

Thames Water supplies water to about 12 million people – almost twenty per cent of the UK's population. Half of these people live in London. The company has to plan ahead for water that will be needed in the future. It has to consider ways of increasing the supply of water and ways of reducing demand. Box C outlines some of the options that it has considered.

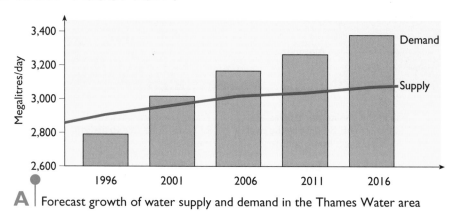

A Forecast growth of water supply and demand in the Thames Water area

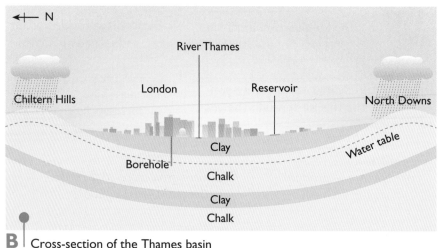

B Cross-section of the Thames basin

- **Desalination** – remove salt from seawater to produce fresh water. There is an unlimited supply, but this is very expensive to do.
- Groundwater development – take more water from aquifers via **boreholes**. Beneath London, the water table in the chalk is rising, as industry uses less water than it used to.
- Leakage control – repair and renew pipes to reduce the number of leaks. This is relatively cheap and could increase supply by up to twenty per cent.
- Water meters – install water meters in homes to encourage people to use less water. Major users, such as industry, already use meters. Metering in homes cuts water use by about ten per cent.

- Icebergs – tow icebergs from the Arctic Ocean to Britain, where they could be melted to provide fresh water.
- Inter-regional transfer – bring water from the wet West and North-west to the dry South-east. One suggestion is a tunnel to transfer water from the River Severn to the River Thames.
- Water conservation – encourage people to save water, for example by collecting rainwater for watering gardens.
- Reservoir – build a new reservoir, so that more river water can be stored and used when needed.
- Recycled water – return more used water to rivers, reservoirs or groundwater, so that it can be reused.

C Options for meeting future demand for water in the Thames Water area

D One of London's many reservoirs

Reservoirs help to supply much of our water. They do this in two ways. Firstly, water can be taken directly from the reservoir and piped to where it is needed. Secondly, reservoirs can be used to store water from the river when the flow is high. This can be released back into the river when the flow is low to supply water further downstream.

Thames Water has proposed that a new reservoir be built near Abingdon in Oxfordshire. This would serve both functions: it would supply water directly to the Upper Thames area and would also release water into the river to increase supply to the Lower Thames area.

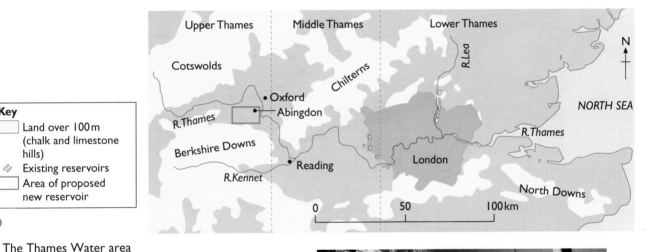

Key
- Land over 100 m (chalk and limestone hills)
- Existing reservoirs
- Area of proposed new reservoir

E The Thames Water area

Activities

1 Look at graph A.
   a) Describe the changes forecast in the supply and demand for water in the Thames Water area. When does demand outstrip supply?
   b) A new reservoir could supply an extra 300 megalitres (Ml) of water per day, but it would take ten years to complete. Will it be able to meet demand? What problems can you foresee?

2 Look at drawing B.
   a) Explain why there is water in the rock beneath London. How is it trapped underground?
   b) Suggest how water could be obtained from this source.

3 Look at the options in box C.
   a) For each option suggest at least one advantage and one disadvantage.

F The new London water ring main, built to replace leaking pipes that were over one hundred years old

   b) Which option would you choose? Give reasons.

4 Look at photo D and map E.
   a) Describe the location of the reservoirs in the Thames Water area.
   b) Explain why they may be located here.
   c) Suggest two reasons for the location of the site for the proposed new reservoir.

G Map extract of the Abingdon area. Thames Water proposes to site a new reservoir within this area. Reproduced from the 1997 1:50,000 Ordnance Survey map by permission of the Controller of HMSO © Crown Copyright.

Should the reservoir be built?

Everybody uses water, but nobody wants to have their home flooded to build a new reservoir. Thames Water has identified an area near Abingdon as the location for a new reservoir but local people are strongly opposed to the scheme. Most of the area lies on impermeable clay that would provide a suitable base for storing water. But the company considers many other factors when choosing the best site for a reservoir. These are listed in box H.

Activities

1 Read the factors in box H.

   Think about how a new reservoir could affect people living in the area. List all the problems it would cause. Can you think of any benefits for local people?

2 Work with a partner.

   a) On a piece of paper, draw a circle with a radius of 2 cm and cut it out. This will represent the reservoir that Thames Water wants to build (on a 1:50,000 OS map 2 cm = 1 km). Work out the real area your circle represents.

   b) Place your circle on map G. By moving the circle around the map, choose the best site for a reservoir. Consider all the factors in box H when you make your choice. (It may not be possible to find a site that meets every requirement.)

   c) On an outline map, draw the reservoir at the site you have chosen. Highlight any buildings, roads, rivers, etc. that may be affected by the reservoir.

   d) Write a short report to explain why you chose this site.

- It should be no more than 5 kilometres from the River Thames, to minimise costs of transferring water.
- To store the amount of water required, it should be at least 3 km² in area, and could be as big as 9 km².
- It should avoid land over 70 metres as this is likely to be limestone (a permeable rock).
- It should avoid rivers and streams. Building here could cause flooding upstream or downstream.
- It should avoid towns and villages. Moving people from their homes is costly and angers people.
- It should avoid main roads and railways. However, it would be an advantage to be close to transport routes during the building.
- It should avoid electricity transmission lines so as not to disrupt power supplies.
- It should avoid airfields and a 4-kilometre radius around them. Reservoirs attract birds, which are a hazard for low-flying aircraft.

H Factors in choosing a site for a reservoir

Assignment

Should there be a new reservoir near Abingdon?

Before a major new development such as a reservoir can be built, there is often a public enquiry to hear all the arguments for and against the proposed development. Then it is decided whether or not to allow the development to go ahead.

   You are going to carry out a public enquiry with the rest of your class into the proposal for a reservoir near Abingdon. You could use the most popular site from activity 2 above.

1 Work with a small group of pupils. Each group will represent one of the interest groups in the box on the right at the enquiry. With your group, decide whether you are for or against the reservoir proposal and why.

Thames Water Company   The Environment Agency
Friends of the Earth   National Farmers Union
South-west Oxfordshire Council   village residents
local sailing and fishing clubs

2 Prepare a leaflet to support your case. You could do this with the help of a desk-top publishing package on a computer.

3 Carry out the public enquiry. Your teacher could act as the chairperson. Each group will have an opportunity to present their case.

   At the end, the chairperson has to weigh up all the arguments and make a decision for or against the proposal.

In this Building Block you will investigate how the Colorado River has brought life to the south-west of the USA and the impact this has had on the river itself.

This will also help you with the USA investigation on page 107.

5.5 Is life in the desert sustainable?

You might think that just about anything is possible in the USA. After all, this is the country that sent people to the moon and gave the world Disneyland. So, building cities in the desert should be no problem – should it?

The Colorado River flows for some 2,400 kilometres from the Rocky Mountains to the Gulf of California through the most **arid** corner of the USA. It has, literally, brought life to the desert.

Since the Hoover Dam was built in 1936, the Colorado has become one of the most extensively controlled rivers in the world. Along its course a series of dams, reservoirs, pumping stations and HEP schemes divert its flow, so that the river reaches the sea as a small trickle. The water is taken by means of canals and tunnels to the many towns and cities that have rapidly grown up in the South-west over the past fifty years. But with so much water being taken from it, the Colorado River is in danger of drying up.

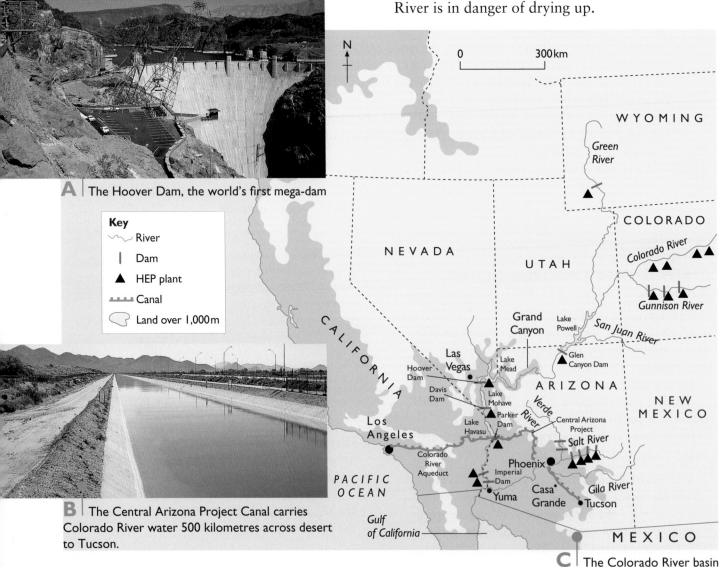

A The Hoover Dam, the world's first mega-dam

Key
~ River
| Dam
▲ HEP plant
⋯ Canal
⬭ Land over 1,000m

B The Central Arizona Project Canal carries Colorado River water 500 kilometres across desert to Tucson.

C The Colorado River basin

> We farm about 1,000 hectares (2,000 acres) in Arizona. That may sound pretty large by UK standards, but around here that is a regular size farm. Our main crop is cotton and we also grow wheat, alfalfa and chickpeas.
> The cotton variety that we grow is well suited to the desert climate of Arizona, but no farming at all would be possible here without irrigation. We water two or three times a week with water from the Central Arizona Project Canal. Until 1992 our water came from wells, but groundwater levels were falling. The CAP was a lifeline. We think it is a more sustainable option and will preserve farming in our valley for future generations. But there have been problems. The water is more expensive and the quality varies – sometimes it can be salty and this damages crops.

D | Paco Ollerton is a farmer near Casa Grande in Arizona with his wife Karen.

	Arizona	USA
Population (millions)	3.8	261
Population density (people per km²)	14	27
Population growth 1985–95 (% per year)	2.9	0.8
Urban population (%)	87.5	76

E | Arizona and the whole of the US compared

F   Irrigated crops on Paco's farm. Agriculture accounts for 90 per cent of water used in Arizona.

Activities

1 Look at photo A.
  a) Find the Hoover Dam on map C. What is the name of the lake it has formed?
  b) What is the nearest city to the Hoover Dam? Suggest two benefits that the dam has brought to the city.
  c) Imagine what the Colorado valley looked like before the dam was built. Draw a sketch.

2 Look at photos A and B, and map C.
  a) List three ways in which people have changed the flow of the Colorado River. Name an example of each.
  b) Explain in what way each of these features could affect the flow of the river.

3 Look at sources D and F.
  a) Explain the importance of irrigation to farming in Arizona.
  b) What advantage does water from the Central Arizona Project Canal have over groundwater supply? What are the disadvantages?

4 Look at table E.
  a) Describe the differences in the population of Arizona compared to the whole of the USA. Can you explain any of these differences?
  b) Suggest how population characteristics in Arizona will affect future demand for water.

Can the Colorado River flow again?

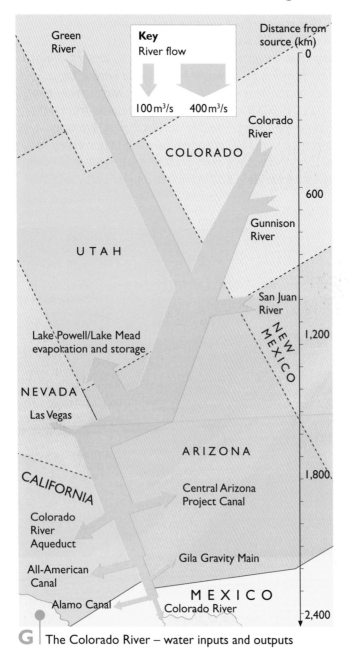

Key
River flow

100 m³/s   400 m³/s

Green River

Colorado River

COLORADO

Distance from source (km)

0

600

Gunnison River

UTAH

San Juan River

1,200

N E W   M E X I C O

Lake Powell/Lake Mead evaporation and storage

NEVADA

Las Vegas

ARIZONA

1,800

CALIFORNIA

Central Arizona Project Canal

Colorado River Aqueduct

Gila Gravity Main

All-American Canal

MEXICO

Alamo Canal   Colorado River

2,400

G The Colorado River – water inputs and outputs

The Colorado River now sustains about 25 million people and 820,000 hectares of irrigated farmland. Arizona is one of the main water-users. It has one of the fastest-growing populations in the USA. When the Central Arizona Project Canal was opened in 1992 it was seen as the solution to the problem of water shortage in the state.

But the project has not gone exactly according to plan. When people in Tucson turned on their taps, water from the canal ruined their plumbing systems: the higher mineral content of the water corroded their pipes. The city has gone back to using groundwater until the problem can be sorted out. Some farmers cannot afford the high price of water from the canal and many of them too have gone back to using groundwater. One of the main aims of the CAP Canal was to restore groundwater levels.

Environmentalists are also concerned about the impact that the canal may have on the Colorado River itself. The river no longer carries so much water or sediment. Already, natural beaches at the bottom of the Grand Canyon have eroded as less sediment is deposited, and along the river fish are disappearing. Some people are recommending drastic measures to restore the Colorado to its natural state (see article J), but then what would happen to the millions of people who depend on the river?

Distance from source (km)	100	300	600	1,200	2,000
River flow (m³/sec)	5	124	409	905	1,003

H Water flow in the Colorado River in 1920 (before any dams or reservoirs were built)

Activities

1 Look at flow map G.
   a) Describe the flow of water in the Colorado River from source to mouth.
   b) How do the inputs to and outputs from the Colorado River help to explain the flow of the river?
   c) List the outputs from the Colorado River. Which of these is the largest? Why is this a problem?

2 Look at table H.
   a) Use the figures to draw a flow map, similar to map G, to show the flow of water along the river in 1920. Give your map two scales to show the distance from the source and the flow in the river.
   b) Compare the flow map you have drawn with map G. Describe the differences that you can see.

I The Grand Canyon, carved from the Arizona desert by the Colorado River over millions of years

August 1997

LET A RIVER RUN THROUGH IT

In the arid West, those who control water control the way the landscape will look. The Colorado River has been the centre of power play over its water resources for decades. But in the zeal to control the river, those fighting for a piece of its watery wealth have virtually ignored the impact on the environment. The developers were very successful in providing water for development of sprawling cities and agriculture, but failed to recognise the long-term unsustainability of the desert kingdom they helped create.

The price for such development has been steep. Today, a disjointed Colorado River system, which bears little resemblance to the historic river, supports more houseboats, jet-skis and ski boats than it does native fish species. Artificially created reservoirs have drowned the cultural heritage of thousands of Native American people who depended on the Colorado River and respected it for the life it provided.

Dams have limited life spans, both structurally and economically. When a dam has lived its useful economic life, or becomes an ecological burden, it is time to make restoration of the river a priority. Today we are at that point with Glen Canyon Dam. Last October a meeting was held in Arizona to raise these issues – the campaign to drain Lake Powell was born.

The Glen Canyon effort would be the largest restoration project ever undertaken in the world. It would be a slow process – it could take ten years to drain the reservoir and years more for sensitive ecosystems to reach their natural balance. It is intended that the dam wall itself remains as an icon to the past, with the river flowing freely around it. It would be a great credit to our civilisation to return the Colorado River to Glen Canyon.

Dave Wegner

J Extract adapted from an article in *World Rivers Review*

Assignment

What future for the Colorado River?

Work in a small group. You have been asked to produce a documentary programme for radio or television about the impact of the Central Arizona Project Canal on the Colorado River. The programme has to explore:

- why the Central Arizona Project was needed
- the benefits and problems the project has brought
- the impact these have had on the Colorado River
- options for the future.

I You should include a short interview with each of the following people as part of your programme:

- a farmer in Arizona
- a resident in Tucson
- a water-resources manager
- a Native American
- an environmentalist working in the Grand Canyon National Park
- a tourist canoeing on the Colorado River.

Each member of the group can play the role of at least one person.

a) Plan the questions you will ask each person.
b) Think about how each person would answer the questions. You could record the interviews.

2 Write a script to link the interviews. Present your programme to the rest of your class.

5.6

Is Africa at a watershed?

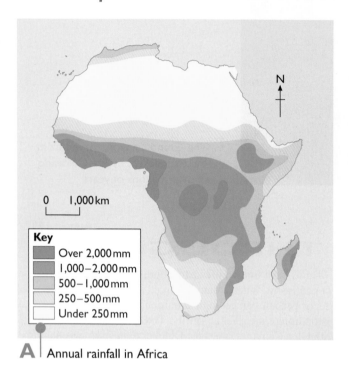

A | Annual rainfall in Africa

Key
- Over 2,000 mm
- 1,000–2,000 mm
- 500–1,000 mm
- 250–500 mm
- Under 250 mm

Half the world's population lacks proper **sanitation**, and more than a billion people have no access to safe drinking water. In many countries, water-related diseases, such as cholera and malaria, are on the increase. The problems of water supply are at their greatest in the LEDCs of Asia and Africa.

Many LEDCs have turned to western solutions to solve their water problems, building mega-dams (see page 94). These promise not only a reliable water supply, but also year-round irrigation for farmers and cheap hydro-electric power to meet growing energy needs. The first LEDC to follow this path was Ghana, where the Akosombo Dam on the River Volta was built in 1964. Since then, many other countries have also built dams, usually funded by aid from MEDCs.

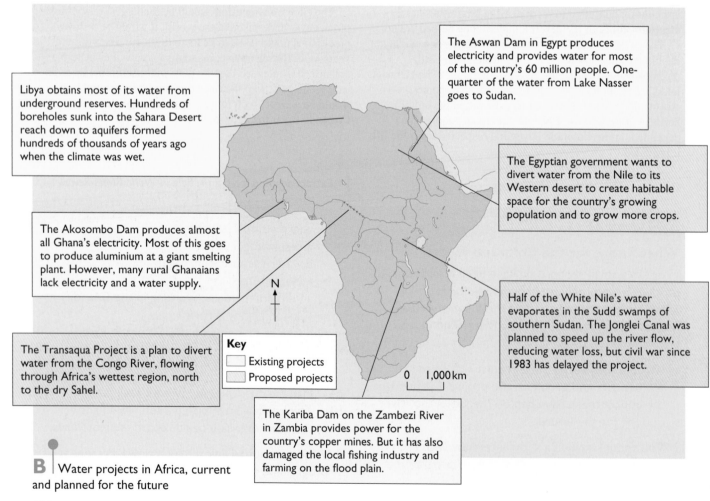

Libya obtains most of its water from underground reserves. Hundreds of boreholes sunk into the Sahara Desert reach down to aquifers formed hundreds of thousands of years ago when the climate was wet.

The Aswan Dam in Egypt produces electricity and provides water for most of the country's 60 million people. One-quarter of the water from Lake Nasser goes to Sudan.

The Egyptian government wants to divert water from the Nile to its Western desert to create habitable space for the country's growing population and to grow more crops.

The Akosombo Dam produces almost all Ghana's electricity. Most of this goes to produce aluminium at a giant smelting plant. However, many rural Ghanaians lack electricity and a water supply.

Half of the White Nile's water evaporates in the Sudd swamps of southern Sudan. The Jonglei Canal was planned to speed up the river flow, reducing water loss, but civil war since 1983 has delayed the project.

The Transaqua Project is a plan to divert water from the Congo River, flowing through Africa's wettest region, north to the dry Sahel.

Key
- Existing projects
- Proposed projects

The Kariba Dam on the Zambezi River in Zambia provides power for the country's copper mines. But it has also damaged the local fishing industry and farming on the flood plain.

B | Water projects in Africa, current and planned for the future

Are large-scale dams the best solution to water problems in Africa? Or is there technology more appropriate to the needs of LEDCs? (You may have looked at the question of appropriate aid on page 31.) The promised benefits of large dam projects do not always happen. Often they fail to help the majority of the poorest people, many of whom may have lost land when the new reservoir was created. And mega-dams like the Aswan Dam can also create environmental problems of their own (look back to pages 94–5).

C People collect water from a village well in Mozambique. The well was built with money provided by an aid agency. A project like this costs only a tiny fraction of the cost of a major aid project like a dam. The well pumps groundwater to the surface and saves women a long walk to collect water from a river. It also provides a reliable source of water with which they can irrigate their crops, so improving yields.

D In Sudan earth basins are a low-cost alternative to mega-dams and can be easily made by farmers. The basins prevent rainwater from running away and eroding the soil. The water is retained and drains slowly into the soil so that it stays moist for longer. Each basin is surrounded by a small earth ridge made with a hoe.

Activities

1 Look at maps A and B.
   a) Compare maps A and B. Which parts of Africa are most likely to suffer from drought?
   b) How does the rainfall pattern on map A help to explain the distribution of rivers on map B?
   c) From map B, consider three proposals for future projects in Africa. Suggest any environmental problems that could arise from each one.

2 Look at photos C and D.
   a) Describe the technology that has been used in each of the water projects shown.
   b) In what ways is this technology 'appropriate' to the needs of LEDCs like Mozambique and Sudan?

3 Imagine that you have been asked to assess two proposed aid projects in an African country that suffers from water shortage.
   • One project involves building a mega-dam like the Aswan Dam (photo B on page 94).
   • The other project involves a range of small-scale schemes in rural areas to relieve water shortage, like those in photos C and D.
   a) Look back at the rules for aid that you devised in activity 4 on page 31. Assess the two projects according to these rules.
   b) Decide which project you would recommend. Give six reasons to support your decision.

Can water wars be avoided?

One of the biggest threats to world peace in the 21st century could be water shortages. Many water sources, including major river and groundwater stores, overlap international boundaries. Disputes arise over water ownership, particularly when one country's actions affect another country's water supply. One area of great tension is northern Africa, one of the world's driest regions.

Egypt relies on the Nile's water and has plans to increase the amount it uses. These plans are threatened by other countries along the Nile who want to increase their share of the water. Eighty per cent of the Nile's water comes from Ethiopia. The country is recovering from a long civil war and plans to build a series of dams and HEP schemes on the Blue Nile and Atbara rivers. The remaining twenty per cent of the Nile's water flows along the White Nile through Uganda and Sudan. Both countries need to increase their supply of water. If the countries along the Nile do not come to an agreement about how to use the water, there is a possibility that tensions could turn to war.

Assignment

How should the Nile be shared?

Work in a group of four. Each person will represent one of the countries along the River Nile: Egypt, Ethiopia, Sudan and Uganda. Map A on page 94 shows the whole region as well as rainfall at different points on the Nile.

1 Study the data in chart E for the country you represent. Decide how the country could improve its water and power supplies in future.
   How could the River Nile help to meet demand? Are there any alternatives to building large dams? How would the country pay for the schemes?

2 Hold a meeting with representatives of the three other countries to negotiate how water from the River Nile should be shared.
   What percentage of the Nile's water should each country use? Do you all agree?

3 Write a report on the meeting. Explain the views of each country, and how you came to your final decision.

Egypt
Area: 995,000 km²
Population: 1996 – 59 million
            2010 (estimate) – 74 million
GNP per capita: $1,080
Life expectancy: M – 64   F – 67
Population with access to sanitation: 11%
Population with access to safe water: 64%
Electricity consumption per person: 896 kilowatt-hours

Ethiopia
Area: 1,000,000 km²
Population: 1996 – 58 million
            2010 (estimate) – 89 million
GNP per capita: $100
Life expectancy: M – 48   F – 51
Population with access to sanitation: 10%
Population with access to safe water: 27%
Electricity consumption per person: 22 kilowatt-hours

Sudan
Area: 2,376,000 km²
Population: 1996 – 27 million
            2010 (estimate) – 37 million
GNP per capita: $400
Life expectancy: M – 53   F – 56
Population with access to sanitation: 22%
Population with access to safe water: 50%
Electricity consumption per person: 37 kilowatt-hours

Uganda
Area: 200,000 km²
Population: 1996 – 20 million
            2010 (estimate) – 27 million
GNP per capita: $300
Life expectancy: M – 43   F – 43
Population with access to sanitation: 57%
Population with access to safe water: 38%
Electricity consumption per person: no data

E

THE USA – Your investigation

In each of Units 1–5, one Building Block investigation has been based on a case study from the USA. You are going to use a range of information, from this book and elsewhere, to investigate an aspect of life in the USA. The map and the photos on this page will remind you of the places that you have already studied.

The USA – your investigation

1 Think of questions about the USA that you would like to investigate, or think of a hypothesis you could test.

For example:
- Which is the best part of the USA to live in?
  or
- Does the USA use its money wisely?

You can probably think of many more. Choose one question that it will be possible to investigate with the resources that you have, and in the time you will be given. For example, if your question was 'Which is the best part of the USA to live in?', you could compare California and Michigan using case studies from this book. Check the question you choose with your teacher before you start your investigation.

2 Plan how you will carry out the investigation. What evidence do you need to find? Where will you find it?
    Think about the resources that you will need to use: this book, an atlas, the library, newspapers and TV, the Internet, personal contacts in the USA, etc. Decide what tasks you will need to do. Check your plans for the investigation with your teacher before you go any further.

3 Collect the evidence from each of the sources that you decide to use. Think of the best way to present your evidence – in the form of maps, graphs, tables, etc. Make sure you don't forget the question that you want to investigate. What does the evidence tell you? If it doesn't help the investigation you probably don't need it.

4 Write up your investigation.

Example: Investigate the question, 'Does the USA use its money wisely?'

- First, think about your own priorities for development, e.g. housing, education, water supply, environment, etc. Make a list in order of importance.
- Compare your priorities with the way money is spent in the USA. Use the USA Building Blocks in Units 1–5 to help you. What was money spent on? In what ways does

this improve the quality of life? In what ways does it make it worse? Find out more about the quality of life in the USA from films, TV or family and friends who live there.
- Finally, compare the USA to other countries using data from pages 34–5. In particular, compare the USA to countries with similar wealth, e.g. Japan, France, the UK. In what ways is the quality of life in the USA better or worse than in any of these countries?

BRINGING TOGETHER

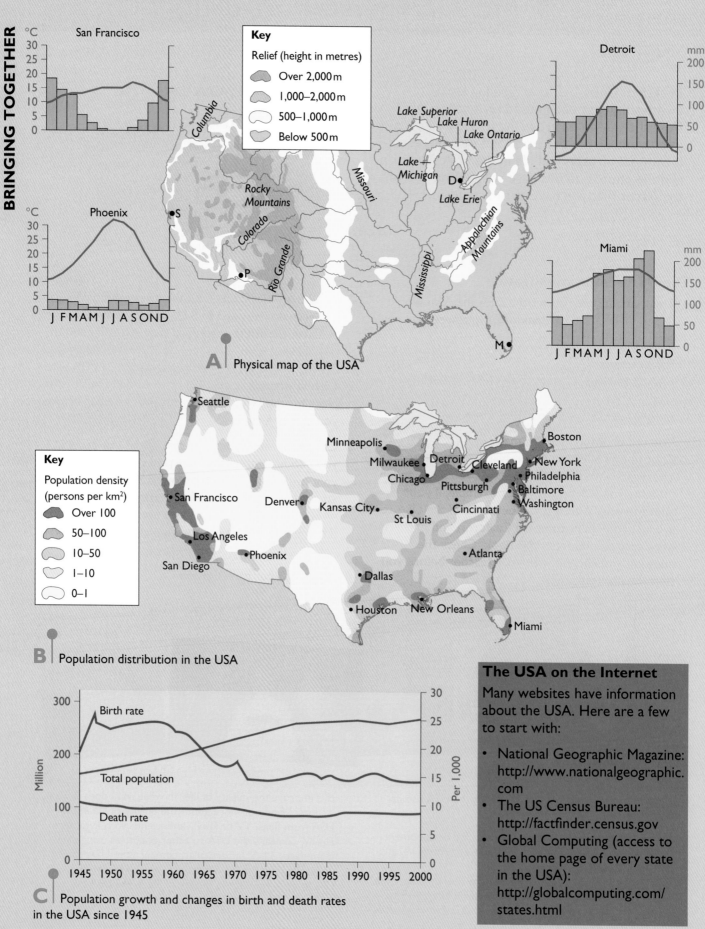

°C San Francisco

°C Phoenix

J F M A M J J A S O N D

Key

Relief (height in metres)

Over 2,000 m

1,000–2,000 m

500–1,000 m

Below 500 m

Detroit mm

Miami mm

J F M A M J J A S O N D

Lake Superior
Lake Huron
Lake Ontario
Lake Michigan
Lake Erie
Columbia
Rocky Mountains
Missouri
Colorado
Rio Grande
Mississippi
Appalachian Mountains

S
P
D
M

A Physical map of the USA

Key

Population density (persons per km²)

Over 100

50–100

10–50

1–10

0–1

Seattle
Minneapolis
Milwaukee
Detroit
Cleveland
Boston
New York
Chicago
Pittsburgh
Philadelphia
Baltimore
Washington
San Francisco
Denver
Kansas City
St Louis
Cincinnati
Los Angeles
Phoenix
San Diego
Dallas
Atlanta
Houston
New Orleans
Miami

B Population distribution in the USA

Birth rate

Total population

Death rate

Million

Per 1,000

1945 1950 1955 1960 1965 1970 1975 1980 1985 1990 1995 2000

C Population growth and changes in birth and death rates in the USA since 1945

The USA on the Internet

Many websites have information about the USA. Here are a few to start with:

- National Geographic Magazine: http://www.nationalgeographic.com
- The US Census Bureau: http://factfinder.census.gov
- Global Computing (access to the home page of every state in the USA): http://globalcomputing.com/states.html

D Population change in the USA, by state, 1990–2000

E Wealth in the USA

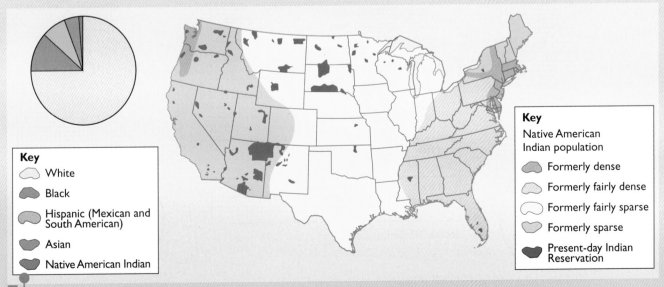

F Ethnic groups in the USA

BRINGING TOGETHER

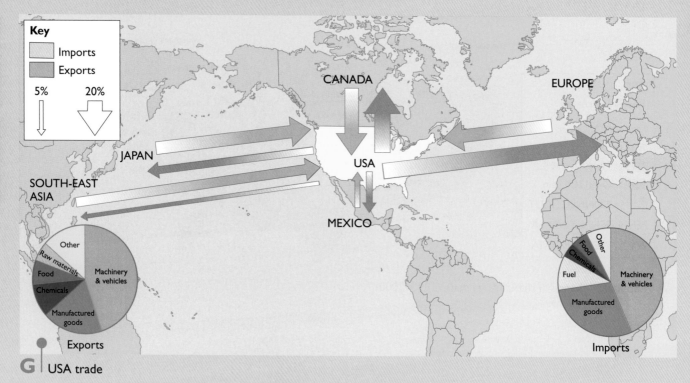

G USA trade

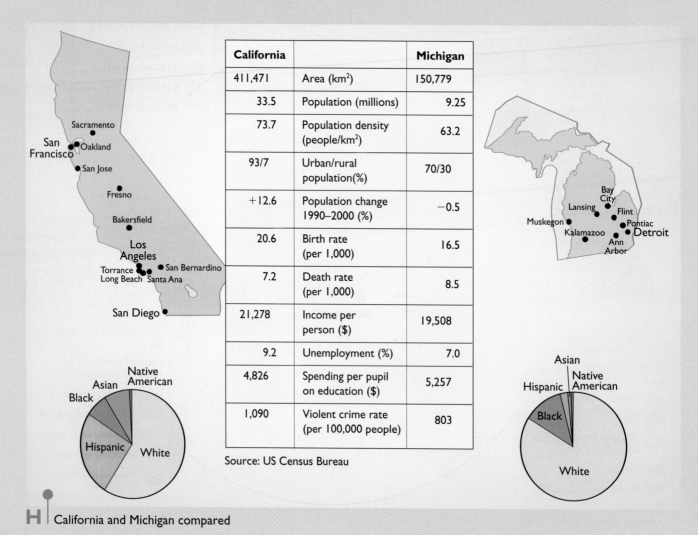

California		Michigan
411,471	Area (km²)	150,779
33.5	Population (millions)	9.25
73.7	Population density (people/km²)	63.2
93/7	Urban/rural population(%)	70/30
+12.6	Population change 1990–2000 (%)	−0.5
20.6	Birth rate (per 1,000)	16.5
7.2	Death rate (per 1,000)	8.5
21,278	Income per person ($)	19,508
9.2	Unemployment (%)	7.0
4,826	Spending per pupil on education ($)	5,257
1,090	Violent crime rate (per 100,000 people)	803

Source: US Census Bureau

H California and Michigan compared

If there was one country in the world that you would like to visit to learn more about geography, where would it be? For me, it was South Africa. In nearly three years of working on the *Earthworks* series, I'd been all around the UK – from the top of Cairngorm to the tip of Spurn Head; to Bristol, Halifax, Carmarthen and Milton Keynes. I'd dragged my family to France and Mallorca. I'd sent my brother to the USA and a good friend to India and Bangladesh to do my research. I'd got friends all over the world – from Monserrat to China, Australia to Zambia – working for me. But this was the visit I wanted to make myself.

At last I was here. As I sat sheltering from the hot African sun on that first afternoon I had to pinch myself to make sure I wasn't dreaming. I had done all my research thoroughly before I came: I'd read all the right books, I'd seen programmes on TV – I thought I was prepared. Surely, as a geography teacher I knew what to expect – didn't I? But nothing fully prepares you for the experience of really going to a place and meeting the people face to face – not books, not TV, not the Internet, not even your imagination! And South Africa was no exception. Despite everything that I already knew, for the next three weeks I was in turn amazed, shocked, thrilled and appalled at what I found.

The previous night flying over Africa, I was too excited to close my eyes. I felt like a five-year-old on Christmas morning. When dawn broke over the African continent I was the only passenger peering through the window at the back of the plane. The sight was awesome. A huge carpet of brown and green stretched as far as the eye could see, bathed in the orange glow of the rising sun. As the plane began to descend, tiny villages came into view, some totally cut-off, others linked by thin brown lines, straight as rulers, that I took to be roads. Even Johannesburg, as we came in to land, was no more than a large splodge on this vast landscape.

From the map, I had memorised the route from the airport to my guest house before I arrived; Jo'burg's reputation as a city of crime went before it. I knew that if I stopped to look at a map while waiting at traffic lights I was likely to be hijacked at gunpoint (at least, that's what I'd seen on the news). What I couldn't know was that there would be a traffic diversion in the city centre, no signposts to follow and that I would get completely lost (something that geographers are not supposed to do!).

But I made it unscathed, and here I was, sitting in the tranquillity of the walled garden at Melville House in one of the smarter suburbs of the city. Incidentally, garden walls in Jo'burg are often taller than the houses they surround. Many homes have been turned into armed fortresses to protect them from crime. Even in the seclusion of the garden there were clues that I was in Africa. A butterfly as large as a bird flitted past. In a tree, a weaver-bird wrestled with leaves as it built its nest hanging from a branch. Above, angry cumulus clouds bubbled up in the summer heat. I closed my eyes. As I caught up on lost sleep I dreamt of what lay beyond the wall. But not even my wildest dreams could have prepared me for what I was to find …

GROUNDWORK

6.1

Are you sure that this is Africa?

What images come into your mind when you think of Africa? Do you think of desert or rainforest or, perhaps, elephants and giraffes roaming wide open plains? You can find all of these in Africa – and you can find them all in South Africa too. But there is more to Africa than just its landscapes and animals! What about its people? Do you think of people who are rich or poor? Where do these people live? What do they do each day? And – while you are still thinking – where did all your ideas about Africa come from?

Photo A may not be your image of Africa, but this photo was taken in South Africa. And if this is not how you picture Africa, you are not alone. Cosmas Desmond, a South African born in Britain, was surprised at what he found when he first went there.

A Johannesburg, South Africa's largest city

B Father Cosmas Desmond, photographed in 1975 when he was under house arrest for writing a book criticising government policies

> I have very little knowledge of geography. When I arrived in South Africa I expected to hear lions roaring around the airport and then to hack my way through the jungle to my mission station – for I came as a missionary. In my ignorance I thought I was coming to Africa to convert the heathen* black hordes. Instead I found that the jungle was concrete and that the heathen were white.

*heathen: people who are without any religion, or uncivilised

Activities

1 **a)** Write down ten ideas that you have about Africa. Your teacher may have asked you to do this before you started this unit.

   b) Beside each of your ideas, state where you think it came from. The box below may help you.

   > newspaper TV film book Internet magazine
   > friend family school personal experience

   c) Share your ideas with other members of your class. How many of your ideas are the same?

   Did they come from the same place? How accurate do you think they are?

   d) Put your ideas away until you have reached the end of this unit. Then look back at them. How have your ideas changed?

   Can you be sure that this book is accurate?

2 Look at photo A.

   a) What questions would you like to ask about it?

   b) How does the photo compare to your ideas about Africa?

So as part of my research for this book, I visited South Africa. As I travelled around the country I kept thinking: the world in one country! It seemed the ideal place to end a geography course. South Africa had it all:

- an amazing physical landscape, with mountains, desert, forest and a stunning coastline
- people representing the whole human race, living in every imaginable condition, from modern cities to traditional villages
- the extreme wealth of MEDCs and the extreme poverty of LEDCs.

As you study this unit you will be able to review many aspects of your Key Stage 3 course: your understanding of weather and climate, settlement patterns, economic activity and development.

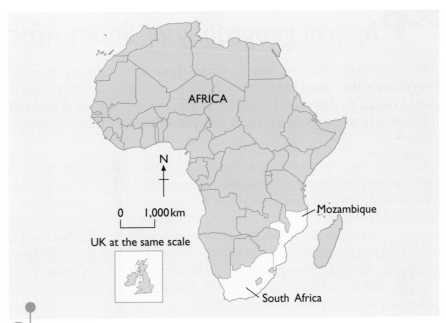

C Africa, showing the UK at the same scale

	UK	South Africa	Mozambique
Population (millions)	58	45	18
Size ('000 km²)	244	1,219	799
Birth rate/Death rate (per 1,000)	13/11	31/9	45/18
Life expectancy (years)	76	63	46
Urban population (%)	89	55	33
Adult literacy (%)	99	81	37
GNP per capita ($)	17,970	2,900	80

D The UK, South Africa and Mozambique compared

3 Read source B.
  a) In what ways were Cosmas Desmond's ideas similar to or different from your ideas about Africa?
  b) What do you think he meant when he said that 'the jungle was concrete and ... the heathen were white'? (You might have more ideas about this question when you have studied more of this unit.)

4 Use map C and table D to compare South Africa with the UK and Mozambique.
  a) Draw graphs to illustrate the data in the table.
  b) For each item in the table, describe the similarities and differences between:

   i) South Africa and the UK
   ii) South Africa and Mozambique (a country more typical of the rest of Africa).
  c) Would it be accurate to call South Africa either an LEDC or an MEDC? Give reasons for your answer.

Homework

5 Look out for news stories about South Africa and other places in Africa on TV or in newspapers.
  a) Keep a record of the stories that you see.
  b) Describe the images of Africa that they show.
  c) How could these images affect our view of Africa?

FRAMEWORK

6.2

Physical geography of South Africa

Africa is a vast continent. South Africa alone is enormous – five times bigger than Britain. But not until I began to drive did I realise just what the difference in scale could mean. A few centimetres on my map could be a whole day's drive! In order to see as much of the country as I could in a short time, I had to fly. The short extracts from my diary in source A describe two flights I took.

As we left the city behind, we were soon flying over endless rolling brown grassland. We crossed a thin black line that must have been a major river. Even at 10,000 metres it became clear the landscape was no longer flat. To my left the brown expanse was broken by hummocks and hollows – hills and valleys in real life. These grew quickly into deep gorges and jagged mountain peaks. We flew over the ridge and the plane descended almost as quickly as the land to the coastal plain.

For most of the flight we hugged the coastline. The deep blue of the ocean was to my left and the whole of South Africa to my right. Compared to the empty interior there was more evidence of habitation. The land beneath was an intricate pattern of settlement, forest, fields and mountains. As we came down to land we caught a glimpse of South Africa's most famous landmark: Table Mountain, perched above the city, with the Atlantic Ocean beyond.

A

B

C | Physical map of South Africa

Key
Land
- Over 2,000 m
- 1,000–2,000 m
- 500–1,000 m
- Below 500 m
- River
- City

ZIMBABWE
BOTSWANA
MOZAMBIQUE
KALAHARI DESERT
NAMIBIA
MMOZAMBIQUE
Pretoria
Soweto Johannesburg
HIGH VELD
SWAZILAND
Vaal
X
Bloemfontein
LESOTHO
Y
Durban
ATLANTIC OCEAN
SOUTH AFRICA
Orange
DRAKENSBURG
INDIAN OCEAN
GREAT KAROO
LITTLE KAROO
East London
Cape Town
Port Elizabeth

D

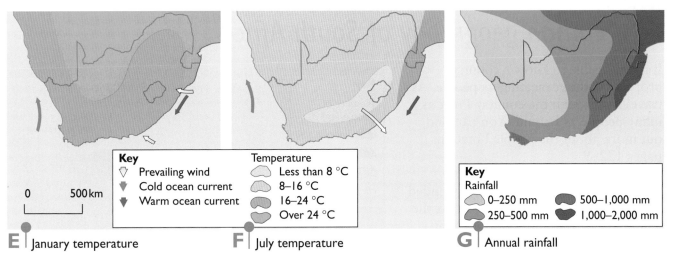

Key

		Temperature	
▽	Prevailing wind		Less than 8 °C
▼	Cold ocean current		8–16 °C
▼	Warm ocean current		16–24 °C
			Over 24 °C

0   500 km

E January temperature

F July temperature

Key

Rainfall

	0–250 mm		500–1,000 mm
	250–500 mm		1,000–2,000 mm

G Annual rainfall

The climate in South Africa is the other way round to what we are used to in Britain. In the southern hemisphere the seasons are reversed. Also, the west of the country is much drier than the east – again the opposite to Britain. This is due to the winds and **ocean currents** that affect the climate.

In summer (January) warm tropical air moves south from the Equator. It meets moist winds blowing from the Indian Ocean over the east of the country. As the air masses converge, warm air is forced up to produce rain, much of it in the form of heavy thunderstorms.

By contrast, cold ocean currents from the Antarctic move up the west coast, cooling the air above so that it carries less moisture and produces little rain.

Activities

1 Read the descriptions in source A and compare them with map C.
  a) Locate the cities on the map where each flight took off and landed. Name the cities.
  b) For each flight, locate the features mentioned in the diary extracts. Name the features.

2 Look at map C.
  a) Draw a large cross-section, like the one below, going from X to Y on the map. On the cross-section, label each of these features:
  Drakensberg mountain range, High Veld, Atlantic Ocean, Indian Ocean.
  b) Mark and label the course of the Orange River onto the cross-section, showing its source and mouth.

X   Y

3 Look at photos B and D.
  a) Describe the vegetation in each photo.

  b) Suggest in which part of the country you would be likely to find each type of vegetation. Use map G to help you.

4 Compare maps E and F.
  a) Describe the differences in temperature between January and July in South Africa.
  b) How do you explain these differences?

5 Look at maps E and G.
  a) Draw the wind direction in January on your cross-section.
  b) Using your cross-section, explain why the west of South Africa is drier than the east.

6 Now, using all the information on these pages, plan your own journey in South Africa.
  a) Describe the route you would choose.
  b) At which time of year would you choose to go? Explain why.
  c) Describe what you would see on your journey. Mention the landscape, vegetation and weather that you would encounter.

FRAMEWORK

6.3 Human geography of South Africa

It is impossible to know a country properly without meeting its people. As I travelled through the country I met as many people as I could. You can find out more about the people I met on pages 122–9.

The majority of South Africa's population is black. They are descended from the groups of people – such as the Khoi-San, Nguni and Tswana – who inhabited this region of Africa before the first white settlers arrived. The white minority are descended from the Dutch who first arrived in 1652, and the British who came some 150 years later. Gradually the white population colonised the land, until eventually they ruled the country.

In the twentieth century the white government established the **apartheid** (meaning 'separate') system that classified people according to their **ethnic group** and made them live in separate areas. People of mixed descent, who did not fit the label black or white, were classified as 'coloured'. South Africa also has an Indian minority descended from people brought from India in the nineteenth century to work on plantations. Although people are no longer made to live in separate areas, you can see from the data in boxes B, C, G and H that quality of life for people in each group is still very different today.

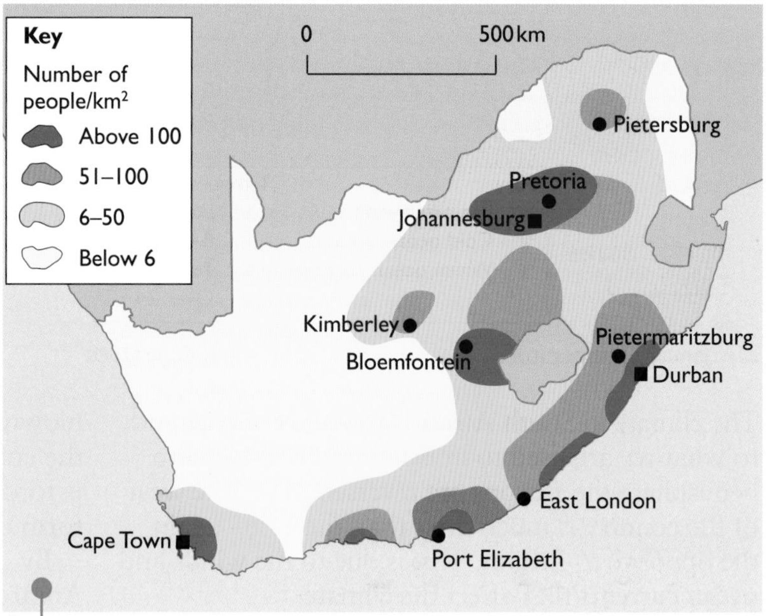
Key
Number of people/km^2
Above 100
51–100
6–50
Below 6
0
500 km
Pietersburg
Pretoria
Johannesburg
Kimberley
Bloemfontein
Pietermaritzburg
Durban
East London
Port Elizabeth
Cape Town

A Population density in South Africa

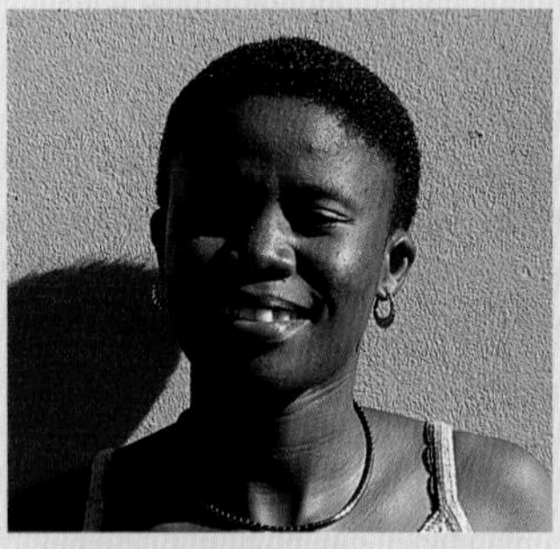

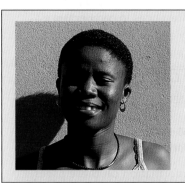

B Black population
Population growth rate: 2.7%
Life expectancy: 60
Years in school: 5.5
Adult literacy: 76.6%
Unemployment: 37%

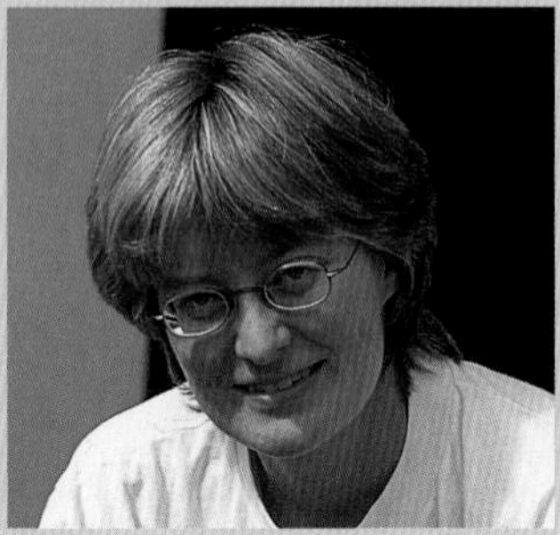

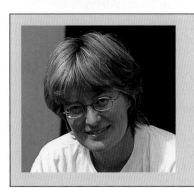

C White population
Population growth rate: 1.2%
Life expectancy: 73
Years in school: 11.7
Adult literacy: 99.5%
Unemployment: 5.5%

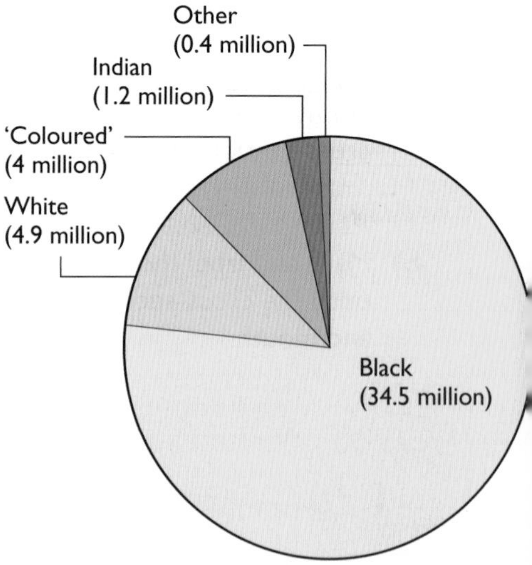
Other (0.4 million)
Indian (1.2 million)
'Coloured' (4 million)
White (4.9 million)
Black (34.5 million)

D Ethnic groups in South Africa

Source: Statistics South Africa, 1998

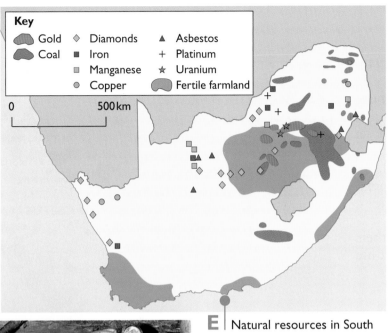

Key

	Gold	◇	Diamonds	▲	Asbestos
	Coal	■	Iron	+	Platinum
		▪	Manganese	★	Uranium
		●	Copper		Fertile farmland

0   500 km

E Natural resources in South Africa

South Africa is rich in natural resources. It has some of the most valuable **mineral resources** anywhere in the world. It is the world's largest producer of gold and platinum, and one of the largest producers of diamonds. It was the discovery of gold in the late nineteenth century that led to the rapid growth of Johannesburg. South Africa also has areas of fertile farmland and is a major exporter of fruit and wine.

F Gold mining in South Africa

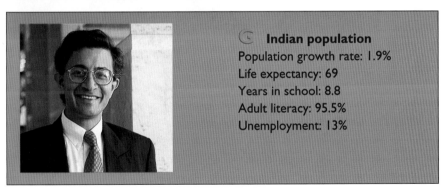

G **Indian population**
Population growth rate: 1.9%
Life expectancy: 69
Years in school: 8.8
Adult literacy: 95.5%
Unemployment: 13%

H **'Coloured' population**
Population growth rate: 1.9%
Life expectancy: 66
Years in school: 6.9
Adult literacy: 91.0%
Unemployment: 22%

Activities

1 Look at map A.
  a) Describe the population distribution in South Africa.
  b) Use map E to help you to explain this distribution.

2 Look at graph D.
  a) Estimate the proportion of each ethnic group in South Africa's population.
  b) i) Compare population growth rate for each group in boxes B, C, G and H.
  ii) Suggest how the composition of the population is likely to change in future.

3 Look at the data about quality of life in boxes B, C, G and H.
  a) Draw graphs to compare:
  i) life expectancy
  ii) years in school
  iii) adult literacy
  iv) unemployment
  for each ethnic group.
  b) Write four sentences comparing the quality of life for different groups of people in South Africa. Use the graphs to help you.

FRAMEWORK

6.4 Division . . .

The apartheid system, made law in 1948, was one of the most unfair forms of government that has ever been dreamt up.

White people owned most of the land, while the remaining areas were set aside as so-called '**homelands**' for the black population (shown in map A). Black people were often forced to move to these 'homelands', which were the poorest land and which could be hundreds of kilometres away from their real homes. (You can find out about life in one of these areas today on pages 126–9.)

However, some black people were needed to work in factories and offices in South Africa's cities. They had to live in **townships** outside the main urban areas. (You can find out about life in a township today on pages 122–5). Others were brought to cities from the 'homelands' as **migrant workers** and had to live in crowded hostels far from their families.

The apartheid system was finally ended in 1994. It shaped the human geography of South Africa, and the divisions it created may take many years to disappear.

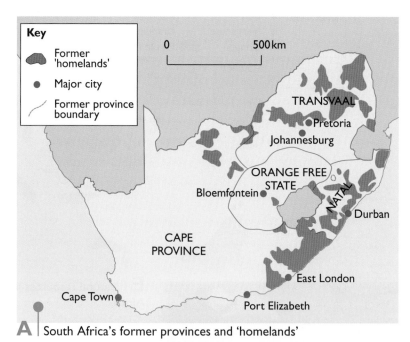

Key
- Former 'homelands'
- ● Major city
- ╱ Former province boundary

0   500km

TRANSVAAL
● Pretoria
● Johannesburg
ORANGE FREE STATE
Bloemfontein ●
NATAL
● Durban
CAPE PROVINCE
East London
Cape Town ●
Port Elizabeth ●

A South Africa's former provinces and 'homelands'

B A migrant workers' hostel in Johannesburg during apartheid

HUURMOTOR STAANPLEK VIR BLANKES

TAXI RANK FOR WHITES.

TAXI WHITE PERSONS

C Apartheid affected almost every area of people's lives. There were even separate public toilets for blacks and whites!

Activities

1 Look at map A.
  a) Estimate the proportion of South Africa that was occupied by 'homelands' for black people.
  What proportion of South Africa was owned by white people?
  b) Compare this with the proportions of black people and white people in the population (see page 116)? How does this show the injustice of apartheid?

2 **a)** Trace every detail of map A onto tracing paper and place it over map E on page 117.
  b) Find out what resources could be found in the black areas and white areas of South Africa. Which cities were in each area?
  c) What does this tell you about the way the country was divided? How would it affect the quality of life for black and white people?

Note: Keep your tracing. You will need it on page 120.

... and development in South Africa

We, the people of South Africa, declare for all our country and the world to know:

That South Africa belongs to all that live in it, black and white, and that no government can justly claim authority unless it is based on the will of the people;

That our people have been robbed of their birthright to land, liberty and peace by a form of government founded on injustice and inequality;

That our country will never be prosperous or free until all our people live in brotherhood, enjoying equal rights and opportunities ...

D Extract from the *South African Freedom Charter*, written in 1955.

Never again shall it be that this beautiful land will experience the oppression of one by another. Let freedom reign. God bless Africa!

E Nelson Mandela spent 27 years in jail because he opposed apartheid. He was president from 1994–99.

3 Look at photo B opposite and photo F on page 117.

Imagine what the life of a migrant gold miner in South Africa would have been like during the days of apartheid. Write a letter to your family, who live in a 'homeland'. Describe:

a) what your life is like

b) your feelings about the apartheid system.

(You can read about the experiences of a former gold miner on page 127.)

4 Read extract D.

a) Suggest what laws the new government in South Africa would have to change to make the country fairer.

As far back as 1912, black South Africans formed the African National Congress (ANC) to oppose the apartheid system. The organisation attracted members from all groups in South Africa, including whites. In the 1960s, after years of peaceful protest, they turned to armed struggle. Many of their leaders, including future president Nelson Mandela, were put in jail for their opposition to apartheid. Hundreds of people died in the years of anti-apartheid struggle.

The apartheid system was not only unfair, it was also an obstacle to development in South Africa. Among the problems it caused:

- many countries refused to trade with South Africa and some large companies would not invest money there
- black people received poor education, so that they lacked the skills and training necessary to work in modern industry
- poor housing and healthcare, especially in the 'homelands', meant that black people suffered poor health, were unable to work and died younger
- separate areas and facilities for blacks and whites were a waste of money and made the country inefficient
- a high proportion of the country's income was spent on defence and policing to keep the apartheid system going.

Eventually, pressure on the government from people in South Africa, as well as other governments, led to the downfall of apartheid. In 1994, for the first time, the whole country was able to vote for a new government. Nelson Mandela was elected the country's first black president.

b) Suggest five priorities for future development in South Africa to overcome the problems created by apartheid.

Homework

5 Find at least one news item about South Africa using newspapers, TV or the Internet. What does it tell you about life in South Africa now? How does this suggest that South Africa has changed since apartheid?

6.5

In this Building Block you will compare the quality of life in different regions in South Africa.

How do regions in South Africa compare?

One of the first changes under the new South African government in 1994 was the creation of nine new provinces, or regions. These replaced four old provinces, as well as the former homelands (see map A on page 118). However, it was difficult to create regions that could share the country's wealth equally. Wealth is still concentrated in the main cities where most industry is located. The poorest areas are still the former homelands, where too many people subsist on low-grade land, with little employment other than farming. For these reasons, inequality still exists between South Africa's new provinces. I chose to visit the new provinces of Gauteng and Eastern Cape, which clearly show some of the contrasts within South Africa.

Activities

1 Compare map A (left) with map A on page 118. Use the tracing you made in activity 2 on page 118 to help you.
   a) Place your tracing on map A. Into which new provinces do the former homelands fall? Which new provinces are the cities in?
   b) Explain how this could affect the quality of life in the new provinces.

A South Africa's provinces

	Percentage of total population	Percentage of total land area	Urban population (%)	Life expectancy (years)	School pupil/ teacher ratio	Adult literacy (%)	Unemployment (%)	Income per person (Rand/ person; R10 = £1 approx.)
Eastern Cape	15.5	13.9	37.3	60.6	41.1	72.3	41.4	4,539
Gauteng	18.9	1.4	96.4	66.0	28.1	92.9	20.9	20,893
KwaZulu Natal	20.3	7.6	43.5	61.5	35.6	84.3	33.1	6,681
Mpumalanga	7.0	6.5	37.3	62.4	36.1	75.5	33.4	10,625
Northern Province	10.9	10.2	11.9	62.7	36.6	73.6	41.0	2,709
Northern Cape	2.0	29.7	71.7	62.7	27.1	79.8	27.2	10,848
Northwest	8.0	9.5	34.8	59.7	30.3	69.5	32.8	6,428
Free State	6.5	10.6	69.6	61.9	34.6	84.4	26.1	8,647
Western Cape	10.9	10.6	89.9	67.7	25.7	94.6	18.6	14,764
South Africa	100.0	100.0	55.4	62.8	33.7	82.2	29.3	9,461

B South Africa's provinces compared
Source: Statistics South Africa, 1998

2 Look at table B.

a) Use the first column to draw a pie chart to show how the population is shared between the provinces.

b) Use the second column to draw a pie chart to show how the land is shared between the provinces.

c) Which is the most densely populated province? Which is most sparsely populated? How can you tell?

3 Look at photos C and D.

a) In what ways do they show inequality within South Africa?

b) Find the data for Gauteng and Eastern Cape in table B. How does the data explain what you can see in the photos?

C Rural Eastern Cape

D Johannesburg (in Gauteng)

Assignment

Which South African province has the best quality of life?

 You are going to compare the quality of life in South Africa's provinces. You could use a spreadsheet programme on a computer to help you to do this.

1 Look at table B.

a) Choose *four* indicators that you think tell you most about people's quality of life.

b) Explain why you chose these indicators.

2 a) Draw a large table like the one below. Rank the four indicators you chose and write them in order of importance in the spaces at the top of each column.

Province \ Indicator	×4	×3	×2	×1	Quality of life score
Eastern Cape					
Gauteng					
KwaZulu Natal					
Mpumalanga					
Northern Province					
Northern Cape					
Northwest					
Free State					
Western Cape					

b) For each of your indicators rank the provinces. Give 9 points to the province that scores best for this indicator down to 1 point for the province that scores worst. For example, if you chose life expectancy: Western Cape (with the highest life expectancy) scores 9, while Northwest (with the lowest life expectancy) scores 1.

Write the scores in the first column on the chart.

c) For each score you give, multiply it by the number at the top of the next column. For example, if life expectancy is your most important indicator, Western Cape's 9 points would give a weighted score of 36 points.

d) Work out the total quality of life score for each province by adding the weighted scores, and write this in the final column.

3 Write a paragraph comparing quality of life in South Africa's provinces. Suggest reasons for the differences.

BUILDING BLOCKS

In this Building Block you will compare the lives of two teenagers in Johannesburg and Soweto, both in Gauteng, and consider how their lives could be improved.

6.6 Can the city be united?

Nomoya Khambule

I live in Soweto. I think it is a cool place to live, but I know it is dangerous, as well. There are seven people living in our house: my grandparents, my aunt and four children, including me. We live in a single-storey house with three rooms: a kitchen, a living-room and a bedroom. We have built an extension with two more bedrooms. I share my room with my little sister. As you can imagine it is a bit crowded, but compared to some families we are lucky.

I live here rather than with my mother because it is closer to my school. My grandparents help to pay my school fees. They both work — grandad is an engineer and grandma is a nursery teacher. We don't have a car. Like nearly everyone in Soweto, we travel by taxi. Our taxis are minibuses that stop whenever you need to get on or off. Sometimes they get very crowded, but it's the cheapest way to travel.

Soweto is a huge township on the outskirts of Johannesburg (the name Soweto stands for South Western Townships). Over 4 million people live here. It was built during the apartheid years to house black workers who were needed to work in Johannesburg, but were not allowed to live there. The township offers little employment for people, since most jobs are in the city. The unemployment rate is almost 50 per cent.

Nearly all Soweto's residents are black. The area where Nomoya lives is fairly typical, neither rich nor poor by Sowetan standards. Some people can afford to move to the richer suburbs of Johannesburg, but they often move back.

However, Soweto also has a shortage of proper housing. Many families live in small cramped houses, and others build their own shacks on areas of spare land. These are called **informal settlements**.

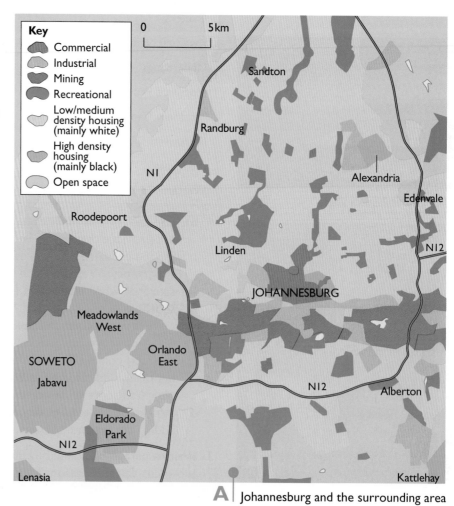

A Johannesburg and the surrounding area

I live in Linden, a suburb of Johannesburg. I live with my mother and her partner, Mark. I am an only child. We own a four-bedroom house with a nice garden. We used to live in a flat, but we moved here because there is more space. We keep two dogs, so that I'm never alone when I'm at home. I do a lot of sport at school, mainly football, athletics and swimming, but my mum doesn't like me going out on my own. She is very worried about crime.

My mother works for a large bank in Sandton – another Johannesburg suburb – and Mark has a job with an insurance company in the city centre. They drive their own cars to work. Because they are both so busy, we employ a housemaid. She lives here during the week and goes back to her family in Soweto at the weekend. We also have a gardener.

Paulo de Almeida

B | Jabavu, the area in Soweto where Nomoya lives

C | Linden, the area in Johannesburg where Paulo lives

Activities

1 Study the information on these two pages about life in Gauteng.
   a) Which person has a lifestyle most like your own? In what ways is it similar? In what ways is it different?
   b) Is the lifestyle of the other person similar to yours in any ways?

2 Look at map A.
   a) Find the location of the two teenagers' homes. Describe the distribution of mainly white and mainly black residential areas on the map.
   b) Compare the land-use pattern in Johannesburg with the pattern in a typical British city (see the map of Bristol on page 48). What similarities and what differences do you notice? Think about the location of areas of high- and low-density housing, industry, and so on.
   c) How can you explain any of these differences?

3 Look at photos B and C.
   a) Describe the density and the pattern of housing in the two areas. How do they compare with the area where you live?
   b) From the photos, draw a simple sketch map of each area to show differences in the housing pattern and density.

4 Most white people in Johannesburg have never visited a township. However, many black people know both types of area well, since they live in one and work in another.
   Imagine that you are the housemaid working for Paulo's family.
   a) Describe your weekly routine.
   b) Describe the contrasts between the two different worlds you live in.
   c) What are your feelings about all of this?

Education for the future

Education may be the most important factor in South Africa's future development. Under the apartheid system, education for black children was very limited. Since they were excluded from the best jobs, the government did not think it necessary to provide them with a good education. As a result, many rebelled and did not go to school at all. Today, black adults are less likely to be literate and more likely to be unemployed than white people.

But old patterns are slow to change. Black children today are still more likely to be taught in old, overcrowded schools and in larger classes than white children. Even in the fairer new South Africa, people with money can opt for better education by paying more to send their children to private school.

D St Matthew's High School, Nomoya's school in Soweto

		Black South Africans	White South Africans
Average number of years in school		5.5	11.7
Number of people (over the age of 20) ('000s):	**With no education**	2,640	8
	Leaving school by the age of 14	1,516	14
	Leaving school by the age of 18	2,110	1,545
	With a university degree	188	403
Adult literacy (%)		76.6	99.5
Unemployment (%)		37	5.5

E Education for black and white South Africans
Source: Statistics South Africa, 1998

F De la Salle Holy Cross College, Paulo's school in Linden

Activities

1 a) What do photos D and F show about the quality of education in the two schools?
   b) From your own experience of school, what factors affect the quality of education?
      Think of at least ten. List them in order of importance.
   c) Explain why you put your top three in this position.

2 Look at table E.
   a) Write five sentences to compare the educational experience of black pupils and white pupils in South Africa.

   b) Explain how education would affect:
      i) the adult literacy rate
      ii) the unemployment rate for each group.
   c) Do you agree that education will be 'the most important factor in South Africa's future development'? Give reasons for your answer.

3 Study the information on the opposite page.
   a) Describe the effect that crime has on people living in Johannesburg.
   b) From what you already know about the city, suggest why the crime rate is so high.

United against crime?

9 September 1997

GAUTENG – CRIME CAPITAL OF SOUTH AFRICA

A new report published today confirms what most people in Johannesburg already know – that crime in the city is at an all-time high. According to the report, compiled by the Human Sciences Research Council, Gauteng Province – which includes both Johannesburg and the capital, Pretoria – has the highest crime rate in South Africa. Seventy-eight per cent of all car hijackings in the country happened in Gauteng, and the number is increasing. The report describes the distribution of six major types of crime within the region: murder, rape, robbery, assault, burglary and motor vehicle theft. Police hope that the patterns shown up in the report will help them to tackle crime more effectively. Hillbrow, near the centre of Johannesburg, has the highest murder rate – not just in South Africa, but the world!

But people in the city are not waiting for police methods to improve. Almost without exception, residents of Johannesburg's northern suburbs now rely on private security firms for protection from crime. Burglary rates in these areas are down, thanks mainly to electric fences and armed response units. It is estimated that households here now spend more than ten per cent of their income on security measures.

Business, too, is taking action to reduce the impact of crime. This year many companies have closed their offices in Johannesburg city centre, where street crime is high, and have moved out to the suburbs, which they believe are safer.

G Extract adapted from the *Johannesburg Herald*

Most people in Soweto have been victims of crime. Our house was burgled while my older sister was at home. She was shot and killed. Last week a pupil at school was shot on his way home – just for some money. Sometimes in bed at night I can hear guns firing. It can be scary.

My family are very worried about crime. When we drive in the city we always keep the car doors locked and windows shut. Cars are often hijacked at gunpoint when people are driving. Our house has a security system and a high wall around the garden. Fortunately, we haven't been burgled.

Assignment

How can quality of life in Johannesburg be improved?

Work in a small group. Imagine that you are pupils at one of the two schools in photos D and F. Some groups will represent pupils at a school in Soweto and other groups will represent a school in Johannesburg.

Your teacher has asked you to suggest ways in which life in your area could be improved, especially to reduce the problem of crime.

1 Discuss ideas in your group. Make a note of good ideas that could help to tackle the problem.

2 Listen to the views of pupils from a group at the other school. How many of your ideas are the same? What ideas can you all agree on?

3 Work with a pupil from the other school to produce a joint plan to improve life in Gauteng. It should include ideas from pupils in both schools.

BUILDING BLOCKS

In this Building Block you will investigate some of the problems of living in rural Eastern Cape and how they can be linked to poverty.

6.1

Is there a future in the countryside?

A The Mahlobisa family – Mlungiseleli and Nomaka with their children Thozamani, aged 12, and Nangomso, aged 10 – outside their home

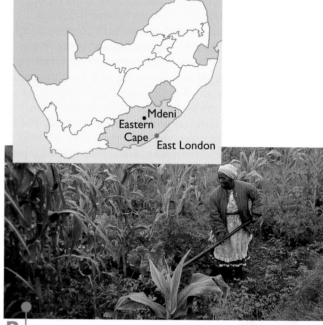

The Mahlobisa family lives in Mdeni, a village in Eastern Cape. It is typical of the many villages scattered over this remote area, known as the Amatole Basin. The area was part of the former 'homeland', called Ciskei. Apartheid may have ended, but little else in Mdeni has changed.

I spent an unusually wet weekend in the village (sometimes the area goes for months without rain). People here seemed much poorer than those living in townships like Soweto. Children played outside in the mud in their bare feet, having little to do indoors. Thozamani and Nangomso could not watch their TV, since it worked from a car battery and that had gone flat. But poverty did not prevent people from providing a warm welcome I will never forget.

The village lies about 150 kilometres from East London, a two-hour drive away. Few people in Mdeni own a car, so they rely on the occasional taxi to travel anywhere. There is little local employment; anyone seeking work has little choice but to go to a city far away from the village. Like many men here, Mlungiseleli was a migrant worker in a gold mine near Johannesburg. He worked there for over thirty years. One day, with no warning, he was told he was no longer needed. Jobless, he has returned to the village, but there is no work here either.

B Nomaka tends the garden that grows much of the family's food. People – often the women – farm land that is too infertile to grow many crops. They keep a few chickens and pigs, and grow vegetables to feed the family. Often there is not enough food and children can be **malnourished** – many appear small for their age.

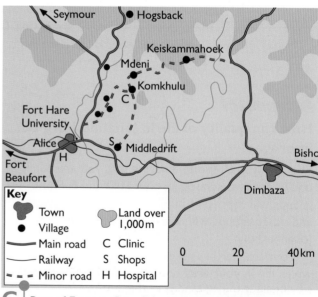

C Part of Eastern Cape Province around Mdeni

My day starts at 7 a.m. I have to light a fire to cook the breakfast. There is no electricity in the village, although the government has promised that there will be one day. At 8 a.m. the children go to school. I spend most of the day working in the garden, collecting firewood and cleaning the house. I built the house myself! I did it with help from my neighbours when my husband was away, working at the mine. I used to spend a lot of time collecting water from the river. Now that we have a tap in the village it is much easier.

No one wants to leave their family, but I had no choice. There was no work for me in Mdeni so when I was younger I went with most of the other men to work in the gold mines. It was hard – and I don't just mean the work. I missed most of the years that my children were growing up. I was able to send some money back to the family, but it wasn't much.

Now I have no work we are poorer. I keep myself busy as chairman of the village Residents' Association. It was the Residents' Association that brought water to the village. We dug a trench all the way from a spring in the mountain down to the village.

We walk to school every day. It is in Komkhulu, a village about 2 kilometres from here. To get there we have to cross the bridge over the river. If it's been raining hard, the river is too dangerous and we can't get to school. Some children have been washed away by the river.

At school we learn Xhosa (our language), Maths and English. It is hard to learn because the classes are big and some children don't behave well. Often the teachers are late. But we are given lunch at school.

D Views and experiences of the Mahlobisa family

Activities

1 Look at map C and photo E.
  a) Describe the location of Mdeni.
  b) Using the map, work out how far people in the village would have to travel to the nearest: i) clinic   ii) hospital   iii) shops.

2 Study all the information on these pages.
  a) List all the problems faced by people living in Mdeni. Think about food, land, housing, employment, health, education, transport and services.
  b) Explain how any of these problems can be linked to the old apartheid system.
  c) i) How has life changed for the family recently?
     ii) How do you think they feel about this?

3 Read what each member of the family says in source D.

   Work in a group of four. Each person should consider one member of the family.

E Children from Mdeni on their way to school

  a) Think about how this person might feel about their life. For example: Nomaka might feel angry that she has to work so hard.
  b) A factory in East London is advertising for new workers. Mlungiseleli must decide whether to apply for a job there. Role play a conversation between members of the family in which they decide what he should do.

Sustainable farming . . .

Parts of Eastern Cape are among the most overpopulated areas of South Africa. People were forced to live in places where there was not enough land to support them and now they cannot afford to move away. Most farms here are very small – too small to produce even enough food to live. Farmers may try to grow more crops or keep more animals than is good for the soil. This, combined with the effect of steep slopes and the droughts that often occur, has led to severe **soil erosion** in some areas.

Overcultivation of crops on too little land exhausts the soil. Eventually nothing will grow and there are no plants to protect the soil.

Overgrazing by livestock quickly removes grass and other vegetation. Bare soil is exposed and easily eroded by wind or rain.

Crop rotation helps soil to recover after crops grow. Crops are moved from one field to another each year while some fields are left fallow.

Terracing fields on hillsides reduces the slope so soil is less likely to be washed away.

Drought causes crops and natural vegetation to die from lack of water. Sudden rain after a drought can wash soil away.

Deforestation happens as people chop down trees for firewood or building. Soil is exposed when trees are removed.

Irrigation can be used to keep soil moist during dry periods and helps crops to grow. Soil is less likely to blow away.

Tree planting helps to protect soil from wind and rain, especially on bare slopes.

F Soil erosion in the Eastern Cape

G Methods of **soil conservation**

Activities

1 Look at photo F.
   a) Draw a labelled sketch to show the effect of soil erosion on the land.
   b) Explain how overpopulation in Eastern Cape could be making the soil erosion worse.
   c) Soil erosion in Mdeni is not as bad as in some other areas. Can you suggest why not?

2 Look at drawing G.
   a) Identify each method of soil conservation in the drawing. Draw a sketch to illustrate each of these methods.
   b) Suggest what obstacle there may be to using any of these methods in Eastern Cape.

... and sustainable communities

Rural areas of Eastern Cape, like Mdeni, are stuck in a **poverty trap**. The most able men move away to find work elsewhere because there is no local employment. They leave behind mainly women, children, older people and the disabled, who make up a higher proportion of the population here than in other parts of South Africa. The government believes that one way to break out of the poverty trap is to create employment in rural areas. Around Grahamstown, the Umthathi Training Project has helped to create jobs for people in the surrounding area, like the women in photo H. Many more projects like this will be needed if the area is to provide jobs for everyone who needs employment.

Assignment

How does poverty affect people in Mdeni?

Here are some everyday experiences for people in Mdeni. Each one is linked to poverty in the village.

A	Children in Nono's class do less well than children at her last school in Grahamstown.
B	Phumla can't afford the pump that would help to irrigate the crops in her garden when there is a drought.
C	Sicelo's cattle are falling sick, and the drugs he needs to treat them are not available.
D	Luyolo is drunk again! He and his friends spend long hours hanging around with nothing to do.
E	Zimkita's daughter is malnourished. This makes her tired and she often gets ill.
F	Thandi finds that she has to walk further than she used to, to collect firewood.
G	Onke is eighteen. He is leaving the village to find a job in East London.
H	Asanda is pregnant. She needs to visit the clinic in Ngwangwane for her medical check, but it is too far to walk.
I	Lusanda wants to produce more crops but needs cattle, or a tractor, to plough the soil.

H | Women producing fabrics – part of a new employment project in Eastern Cape

1 Write the word Poverty in the middle of a page.

2 Arrange copies of the everyday events around the page. Try to make links between the events. Place events that are linked next to each other and stick them on the page. For example, A could be linked to E.

3 Draw arrows to show the links between the events and with poverty. Write a sentence on each arrow to explain the link. For example: Children may not do well in school because they are tired.

4 Employment projects could help to create wealth in the village. Draw a similar diagram to the one you have made, but with the word Wealth in the middle. How might each of the events change?

DIGGING DEEPER

6.8

South Africa – the world in one country?

In many ways South Africa is a unique country. Here the wealth and technology found in MEDCs and the poverty typical of most LEDCs exist side by side. You could think of South Africa being like a microcosm, or miniature version, of the whole world. Most of the world's wealth is in the hands of a minority of the population – as it is in South Africa. And the majority of the world's population, outside the few privileged areas, remains poor – as it does in South Africa.

So, how does South Africa compare with the rest of the world? Is it correct to call South Africa 'a microcosm of the world'?

A The 'new' South Africa

Level of development	Human Development Index	Countries and *South African provinces*
High level of development	0.932	Canada
	0.904	UK
	0.836	Singapore
	0.826	*Western Cape*
	0.820	Venezuela
	0.820	*Gauteng*
Medium level of development	0.729	Romania
	0.698	*Northern Cape*
	0.694	*Mpumalanga*
	0.679	Paraguay
	0.677	South Africa
	0.665	Sri Lanka
	0.657	*Free State*
	0.644	China
	0.602	*KwaZulu Natal*
	0.551	Egypt
	0.543	*North West*
	0.513	Swaziland
	0.507	*Eastern Cape*
Low level of development	0.476	Lesotho
	0.474	Zimbabwe
	0.470	*Northern Province*
	0.252	Mozambique

B Levels of development according to the UN Human Development Index, comparing South Africa and its provinces with other countries.

The HDI goes from 0 to 1. A country with an HDI of 0 would be completely undeveloped. A country with an HDI of 1 would be completely developed. All countries fall between these two extremes.

Source: Statistics South Africa, 1998

Activities

1 Look at cartoon A.
Explain what you think the cartoon is trying to say.

2 Look at table B.
a) What does the UN Human Development Index measure? (Look back at page 34 if you need reminding.)
b) Where does South Africa rank among other countries? Does this surprise you? Why?
c) Which South African provinces rank above the national average? Which fall below?
d) Compare the rank order in this table with the order that you found in activity 2 on page 121. Was it similar? Why?

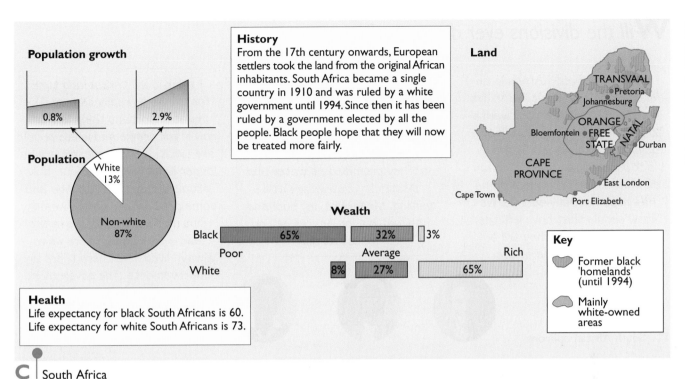

C | South Africa

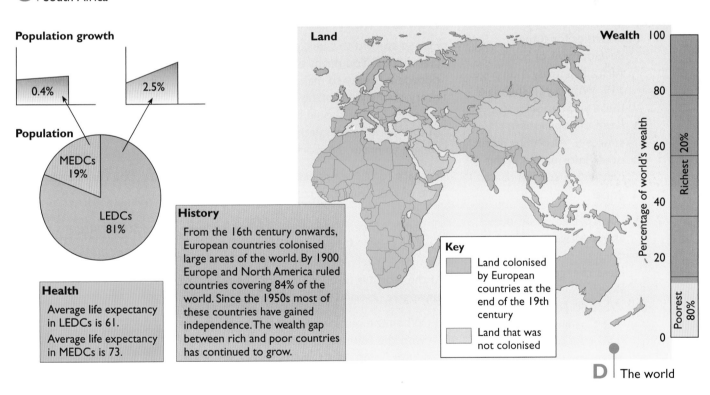

D | The world

3 Work in a group of up to five people.
 a) Each person should study the data under one of the headings in boxes C and D. What are the similarities? Are there any differences? Write a paragraph to compare the data for South Africa and the whole world.

 b) Share the information with your group. Think about ways in which the information under different headings could be linked.

4 With your group, discuss the statement, 'South Africa is a microcosm of the world.' To what extent do you think the statement is true or false?

DIGGING DEEPER

Will the divisions ever disappear?

> I agree that South Africa is an unfair place. I wouldn't like to live in a township. But no one wants to give up what they have. If the government gives more jobs to black people that could be unfair on whites. The problem of crime has become really serious. We know people that have left the country because they are so worried about the future.

> The new government has made no difference to us. We are worse off now than we were before. Because we live so far from the city, the politicians forget about us. They promised us water and electricity, but we are still waiting. Meanwhile, my husband has lost his job and we get no money at all.

> I think it will take a long time for things to really change. The most important thing is that now black people and white people are treated the same. We are no longer judged by our colour. Black people can get decent jobs and some are becoming more wealthy. But most of us still live in the same townships where we've always lived. Even here there are improvements. The government has provided water, electricity and sanitation in the poorest areas.

E | South African opinions

Activities

1 a) Look back at your priorities for future development of South Africa in activity 4 on page 119. Would you still make these your priorities?

b) Read the opinions in source E. Also think about other information in this unit. What still has to be done?

2 a) Look back at your ideas about Africa in activity 1 on page 112. Have your ideas changed? In what ways?

b) What do you now think that Cosmas Desmond meant when he said 'the jungle was concrete and ... the heathen were white'?
Do you agree with him? Give reasons.

Assignment

How can we create a fairer world?

Having studied this unit you will know that South Africa is a country of inequalities. You might think that it should be much fairer. From the outside it is easy to make judgements like this, but there is inequality in every country, including our own. And, if South Africa is a microcosm of the world, what should be done about global inequality? Britain is part of the world's rich minority. Are you willing to give up part of your wealth to make the world a fairer place?

Prepare for a class debate on the issue of inequality. You could choose one of these motions to debate:
Either
'If South Africa is to become a fairer country, white South Africans must give up some of their wealth.'
Or
'If the world is to become fairer, people in rich countries, like Britain, must give up some of their wealth.'

1 When the motion has been chosen, decide whether or not you agree with the statement. Think about what you found out in this unit about South Africa and in Unit 2 about development.

2 Write a short speech, to last about two minutes, to make during the debate. Make sure you have evidence to support your points.

3 Debate the motion with your class. Choose someone to act as chairperson – it could be your teacher. Give everyone a chance to make their speech and allow time for questions.
   At the end of the debate, take a vote to find out how many people are for and how many are against the motion.
   If it was up to your class, would the world be a fairer place?

Glossary

acid rain – rain with a higher than average level of acidity, caused by gases that dissolve in moisture in the atmosphere

active volcano – a volcano that has recently erupted

aid – help, in the form of money, food, people or equipment, usually sent by MEDCs to LEDCs

apartheid – the separation of people by their ethnic group, practised in South Africa until 1994

aquifer – a permeable rock that holds water

arid – dry

ash – fine particles of rock thrown from a volcano when it erupts

birth rate – the number of people born each year per 1,000 population

borehole – a hole drilled into rock in order to obtain water

brownfield site – derelict urban land that is used for building

central business district (CBD) – the central part of a town or city where most shops and offices are found

coal-fired power station – a building where coal is burned to produce electricity

colonise – take over land, or territory, and settle there

concentric ring model – a model of the city that shows a series of circular zones growing out from the centre

cone – a circular shape that rises to a point, typical of a volcano

conservation – care for resources and the environment

continental drift – the process by which the world's continents are slowly moving

core – the central part of the Earth, below the mantle

crater – a funnel-shaped hole at the top of a volcano

crust – the thin layer of rock that forms the outer part of the Earth

dam – a structure built to hold back water, forming a reservoir

death rate – the number of people dying each year per 1,000 population

deplete – reduce, for example fossil fuel reserves

derelict – abandoned or unused

desalination – the removal of salt from seawater to produce drinking water

development – improvement in people's quality of life

dormant volcano – a volcano that has not erupted for many years

doughnut effect – the process by which business abandons the CBD to move to out-of-town sites, leaving a 'hole' at the centre

drought – a serious water shortage

earthquake – a sudden violent movement within the Earth's crust

economic boom – an increase in the level of economic activity when more goods are bought and sold

economic growth – an increase in the amount of goods produced, leading to an increase in wealth

emission – something that is given off, for example gas from a car exhaust

energy – power needed to do work

enterprise zone – a redevelopment area where new business is encouraged

epicentre – the point on the surface above the origin of an earthquake

ethnic group – a group of people distinguished by their physical characteristics or language

evacuate – move people from an area of danger

exploit – use, or develop, a resource for people's own benefit

export – sell goods or services to another country

extinct volcano – a volcano that has not erupted within historic times

fair trade – trade that pays a fair price to the farmers who grow the crops

fault – a crack or tear in the Earth's crust

focus – the origin of an earthquake

fossil fuel – a fuel, such as coal or oil, formed from plants or animals buried in the ground

geothermal power – energy from natural heat in rocks

ghetto – part of a city occupied by one ethnic group, often in the poorest area

global warming – the increase in average temperatures that is happening around the world

green belt – countryside around a city where building is restricted by law

greenfield site – rural land that is used for building

greenhouse effect – the way that gases in the atmosphere trap heat from the Sun

gross national product (GNP) – the total value of all the goods and services produced by a country

GNP per capita – GNP divided by population, as a measure of a country's wealth

groundwater – water that collects in rock below ground

heavily indebted poor country (HIPC) – an LEDC where a large proportion of GNP is spent repaying debt

'homeland' – land set aside for the black population in South Africa during the apartheid years

Human Development Index (HDI) – a measure of development used by the United Nations to compare countries

hydro-electric power (HEP) – electricity generated by water power

import – buy goods from another country

infant mortality rate – the number of children who die in their first year of life for every 1,000 born

informal settlement – shanty town, or homes that people build for themselves on empty land

inner city – the area of a city around the city centre

interdependent – countries rely on each other for the goods and services they need

international debt – money owed by countries to international banks and to governments of other countries

irrigation – the supply of water to the land, usually for farming

land-use zone – an area of a city recognised by its main land use, for example the CBD

lava – molten rock from a volcano

less economically developed country (LEDC) – a poorer country with low GNP per capita

life expectancy – the average age that people can expect to live to

long-term aid – aid given to a country over a number of years to support development

magma – molten rock found beneath a volcano

malnourished – lacking the food needed for a healthy diet

mantle – the middle layer of the Earth between the crust and the core

manufactured goods – products from a factory

mid-oceanic ridge – where two plates are moving apart beneath the ocean and magma rises to form new crust

migrant worker – a person who moves away to work, often returning home later

mineral resource – material obtained from rock by mining, for example coal or iron

more economically developed country (MEDC) – a richer country with high GNP per capita

national grid – a network of transmission lines and underground cables carrying electricity across the country

natural hazard – a natural event that cannot be predicted, creating danger for people

natural increase – population growth that happens when the birth rate is higher than the death rate

non-renewable resource – a resource that cannot be replaced when it is used up

nuclear power – energy produced by carrying out a nuclear reaction in a power station

ocean current – the large-scale movement of water that is colder or warmer than the ocean around it

open-cast mining – a method of mining rock where the overlying layers are scraped off

open space – an area without buildings

plate – a large segment of the Earth's crust

plate boundary – the line where two plates meet

plate tectonics – the movement of plates as they float on the molten rock in the mantle beneath

population pyramid – a population graph that shows males and females in each age group

power station – a place where electricity is generated

poverty trap – a cycle of low income, poor health and poor education from which it is hard to escape

primary goods – natural resources produced from the land or sea

primary source – a first-hand source of information

pyroclastic flow – a volcanic cloud of hot ashes and gases moving at high speed down slopes

raw material – something that is used to make a product

recession – a decrease in the level of economic activity when fewer goods are bought and sold

recycle – reuse a resource to reduce waste

redevelop – improve an urban area by demolishing old buildings and replacing them with new ones

refine – purify a natural resource, for example oil in an oil refinery

renewable resource – a resource that can be used over and over again without being used up

reserves – the amount of fuel that remains unused below ground

reservoir – an artificial lake in which water is stored

Richter scale – the scale used to measure the strength of earthquakes

sanitation – a system to dispose of sewage

secondary source – a second-hand source of information

sector model – a model of the city that shows a number of sectors, or wedges, radiating out from the centre

seismic activity – earthquakes and other movements, usually along a fault in the Earth's crust

seismic gap – part of a fault along which there has been no seismic activity

seismometer – an instrument to measure earth movements

shield volcano – a gently sloping volcano that has been formed from runny, fast-flowing lava

shock wave – tremor, or vibration, caused by an earthquake

short-term aid – emergency relief given to a country after a disaster to help it to recover quickly

silt – fine-grained soil often deposited by a river in flood

soil conservation – ways of reducing the process of soil erosion

soil erosion – the removal of soil by wind and water and by movement down slopes

solar power – energy obtained directly from the Sun's rays

spring – a natural source of water found where groundwater comes to the surface

subsidiary cone – a smaller cone that may grow on the side of a larger volcano

suburb – an area near the edge of a town or city that is mainly low-density housing

suburbanisation – the growth of suburbs at the city edge into surrounding rural area

surface water – water that lies on top of, or flows over, the ground

tenure – the conditions under which someone lives in their home (whether they own or rent it)

township – part of a city set aside for non-white groups of people in South Africa during the apartheid years

trade – the movement of goods between producers and consumers, and between countries

tremor – a small earthquake, or vibration, in the Earth's crust

tsunami – a huge wave often caused by an earthquake on the ocean floor

turbine – a motor that turns to create electricity in a power station

Urban Development Corporation (UDC) – an organisation set up to bring about redevelopment in an old inner city area

urban model – a simple way to show the land-use pattern in a city

urban sprawl – the extension of the city into the countryside

vent – a pipe that carries magma to the surface of a volcano

volcanic bomb – a lump of solidified lava thrown from a volcano when it erupts

volcano – a cone-shaped mountain formed from lava and/or ash

water table – the level of water in the ground below which rock is saturated

wind farm – a group of wind turbines used to generate electricity from wind

Index